A SELECTION
OF ARTICLES ON
MAKING LINGERIE

A DRESSMAKER'S GUIDE

BY
ROSE H. THORPE

British Library Cataloguing-in-Publication Data
A catalogue record for this book is available from
the British Library

Dressmaking and Tailoring

Dressmaking and Tailoring broadly refers to those who make, repair or alter clothing for a profession. A dressmaker will traditionally make custom clothing for women, ranging from dresses and blouses to full evening gowns (also historically called a mantua-maker or a modiste). Whereas a tailor will do the same, but usually for men's clothing - especially suits. The terms essentially refer to a specific set of hand and machine sewing skills, as well as pressing techniques that are unique to the construction of traditional clothing. This is separate to 'made to measure', which uses a set of pre-existing patterns. Usually, a bespoke tailored suit or dress will be completely original and unique to the customer, and hence such items have been highly desirable since the trade first appeared in the thirteenth century. The Oxford English Dictionary states that the word 'tailor' first came into usage around the 1290s, and undoubtedly by this point, tailoring guilds, as well as those of cloth merchants and weavers were well established across Europe.

As the tailoring profession has evolved, so too have the methods of tailoring. There are a number of distinctive business models which modern tailors may practice, such as 'local tailoring' where the tailor is met locally, and the garment is produced locally too, 'distance tailoring', where a garment is ordered from an out-of-town tailor, enabling cheaper labour to be used -

which, in practice can now be done on a global scale via e-commerce websites, and a 'travelling tailor', where the man or woman will travel between cities, usually stationing in a luxury hotel to provide the client the same tailoring services they would provide in their local store. These processes are the same for both women's and men's garment making.

Pattern making is a very important part of this profession; the construction of a paper or cardboard template from which the parts of a garment are traced onto fabric before cutting our and assembling. A custom dressmaker (or tailor) frequently employs one of three pattern creation methods; a 'flat-pattern method' which begins with the creation of a sloper or block (a basic pattern for a garment, made to the wearer's measurements), which can then be used to create patterns for many styles of garments, with varying necklines, sleeves, dart placements and so on. Although it is also used for womenswear, the 'drafting method' is more commonly employed in menswear and involves drafting a pattern directly onto pattern paper using a variety of straightedges and curves. Since menswear rarely involves draping, pattern-making is the primary preparation for creating a cut-and-sew woven garment. The third method, the 'pattern draping method' is used when the patternmaker's skill is not matched with the difficulty of the design. It involves creating a muslin mock-up pattern, by pinning fabric directly on a dress form, then transferring the muslin outline and markings onto a paper pattern or using the muslin as the pattern itself.

Dressmaking and tailoring has become a very well respected profession; dressmakers such as Pierre Balmain, Christian Dior, Cristóbal Balenciaga and Coco Chanel have gone on to achieve international acclaim and fashion notoriety. Balmain, known for sophistication and elegance, once said that 'dressmaking is the architecture of movement.' Whilst tailors, due to the nature of their profession - catering to men's fashions, have not garnered such levels of individual fame, areas such as 'Savile Row' in the United Kingdom are today seen as the heart of the trade.

DAINTY LINGERIE

ROSE H. THORPE

ALL through the ages needlework has been the pastime, often the solace, of women. In this enlightened and electrical age, conditions are happier. Science and machinery have combined to take much of drudgery from life. At the same time mechanical control has made the need for creative self-expression more necessary than ever before. Surely there could be no more fitting medium of individual expression for women than fashioning something of loveliness.

Modern underwear as the counterpart of dress is just as susceptible to fashion ; both are equally affected. The significant difference is that dress is first to register change. Lingerie must be subservient. Under no circumstance will interference with the skilfully achieved line of dress be tolerated. The only course is to co-operate. Not only must lingerie conform to line, good taste demands that it be appropriate to the type of garment also, even at times to being made of the same material. This may seem discouraging to the enthusiast eager to carry out her own ideas, but it is not so really. Simplicity and suitability are governing principles in beauty of design, while restraint may prove the needed impetus to invention. The fashioner of lingerie will find ample scope for her talents, many thrills, and much enjoyment for her leisure hours.

THE RIGHT TOOLS. The same tools are required as for plain needlework, including especially :

Sewing Machine. It may seem heresy to suggest machining fine lingerie, but that is only a tradition which dies hard. For most inside stitching the machine is a decided advantage, not only from a time-saving point of view, but because the line is more true and clearly defined.

Scissors. Two pairs. One for cutting out, 7 inches to 8 inches long. Dressmaking shears are unsuitable for flimsy materials. The other pair, small and sharp-pointed, for buttonholes, cutting threads and surplus material from embroidery, etc.

Yard-stick. Necessary to get seam edges straight before sewing.

Pins. These are very important. Plaited brass lillikin pins should be used—steel marks delicate fabrics.

Between Needles. No. 8–10 to carry fine silk and cotton ; thread No. 90–100.

Crewel Needles. No. 8–10 for embroidery thread.

1

Sharps. No. 6–8 for tacking, and No. 1–2 for punching stitches
Wool Needles. Used to turn inside-out narrow shoulder straps, and rouleaux.

Thimble. Smooth so as not to roughen threads and materials. Small rustless press studs, and pearl buttons, No. 14 lines, for fastenings. Tracing wheel stiletto and inch-tape are all indispensable, so also is pressing equipment—soft and well padded to "raise" embroidery. Lastly, a small work apron should be worn during sewing operations. Exquisite daintiness is the end in view !

THE PATTERN. It is not the purpose of this article to initiate into the mysteries of patternmaking, though it is unbelievably simple. Those who have a dress sense and an eye for line may probably fashion their own shapes. The inexperienced will be wise to buy a paper pattern from a firm of repute, or better still, have a few lessons in drafting.

All paper patterns should be tested before use—pinned together, tried on, and necessary alterations made.

MATERIALS. Good material will make good work easy and give greater joy in the doing of it. The most expensive are not necessarily the best materials.

Qualities to look for : (1) Fineness of texture. One way of cheapening a fabric is to have fewer threads to the square inch, and have them coarser ; (2) Evenness of weave ; (3) Flexible, but not harsh, and springy ; (4) Edges which do not fray unduly ; (5) Silk should be lustrous—excepting such makes as georgette. A bright metallic lustre indicates art silk, or metallic loading. The latter is most detrimental to wear.

One must buy with discrimination not only as regards quality but also as to suitability of purpose. Soft clinging materials may be ideal for bed-time wear but disastrous for the frock above if used as a Princess foundation slip.

Colour is important also. A strong colour, for example, is more appropriate when pyjamas are in question than for the more feminine "nightie." While flesh-pink almost suggests camiknickers, unless the covering frock is to be matched. Pastel tones with oyster, ivory and natural are most " safe."

Buy, too, with a thought to laundering. Washing satin will " come up smiling " after repeated tubbings, while crêpe de chine is more apt to get " dejected." On the other hand, crêpe de chine is more easy to manipulate in making-up. French Spun, which has a slight crinkle in the weave, is the ideal spun silk.

MATERIALS TO CHOOSE FROM. Satin Beauté (washing satin with a crêpe de chine back), Crêpe de chine, Lingerie Crêpe, Spun Silk, Georgette, Triple Ninon, Art Silk Crêpe de Chine, and other art silk fabrics if they satisfy the test as to quality and laundering, Voile, Linen-lawn, cambric and cotton materials.

LACE. The choice of lace presents so many pitfalls to the unwary that a few hints may not be out of place.

Real hand-made lace is expensive but not prohibitive, if only a narrow edging is required. Buyers from this class may safely be allowed to indulge their fancies.

Imitation laces are the problem ! Many are excellent, but others are obviously " cheap."

Imitations that are safe to use : Valenciennes, torchon, cluny, blond, Nottingham needle-run lace.

Imitations to avoid : Guipure, filet, needlepoint, including imitation Irish crochet, and usually machine needle-run lace, if the outlining cord is thick, heavy and loosely run.

Qualities to look for : (1) A well-finished edge, with " Val " and blond laces, clearly defined picots as well ; (2) The mesh of the background in hand-made net laces will be slightly irregular owing to the twisting or plaiting of the threads. Reliable imitations have this quality to a lesser degree, but in poor imitations the mesh has a hard, obviously machine-made appearance ; (3) The lace should be made of linen, mercerised or good cotton thread. Inferior cotton is rough and looks " cheap," especially in white.

POINTS IN CUTTING OUT. If the fabric is to be folded other than in the maker's crease, press out the crease and refold as required, measuring to ensure accuracy.

Avoid waste by planning all the pieces on the material before cutting out any one piece. A great deal of satisfaction is got by cutting out economically, especially when the material is expensive.

The selvedge threads should as a rule be directly in the centre of each piece, excepting when cutting on the cross.

Pin freely from the top downwards, but not too close to the edges.

The pattern should be followed implicitly, allowing turnings, or not, as directed. A corner slurred off affects " fit " and " cut."

If the tracing wheel leaves no impression the thumb-nail may prove effective in marking turnings, or faint ticks with a blue pencil may be used. A lead pencil will soil and smudge. Single tacking or thread-marking should be used for darts and yoke positions, etc.

ASSEMBLING THE PARTS. Each section should be completed so far as possible before assembling the whole.

DETAILS THAT COUNT. Beautiful sewing and delicate handling are important factors in fashioning exquisite lingerie. Never experiment on the garment. It is well worth while to try out each new process on a piece of self material.

PIN TUCKS. Tucks are easily worked by the straight warp threads. Their beauty depends upon breadth, regularity of run-

1. Shoulders shirred before joining seams.   2. Tucks.   3. Skirt on to Bodice.
4. Darts first before seams.   5. Yokes.

stitches and even spacing. The name implies breadth of a pin. To make them more means sacrificing daintiness.

They should be measured from fold to fold. Tacking is un-necessary if the grain of the fabric is followed. To define the line a thread may be pulled—but not out ! A quicker aid is to make a small paper gauge. The spacing varies according to the position of the tucks—¼ inch to ⅜ inch is most usual.

SHIRRING. A soft method of dealing with fulness at the shoulders and waist of a garment in silken material.

Several parallel rows of flash-running or very fine run-stitching are worked across by the weft of the material on the right side. The rows must be equi-distant—usually ¼ inch apart. The threads are not fastened off until the garment is assembled. Twice to three times the finished space should be allowed for shirring.

WHIPPING. Occasionally it is necessary to have a finished edge where there is fulness. This method is only suitable for fine materials and is more easy to execute on cambric than silk.

The edge is rolled on to the wrong side and whipped, com-mencing from the right-hand corner. A strong matching thread should be used. The tiny roll should be formed, whipped and pulled up every inch, the needle passing under not through the roll. This method may also be used to make neat an edge without gathering up the material.

VEINING. A delightful method of joining edges to impart a " delicate air." The edges to be connected must first be finished (*see figs.*, *p.* 32) and tacked on to paper with a narrow space between.

Matching or contrasting coloured thread may be used—one strand of filoselle or stranded cotton, or silk from the reel. There are many forms of this stitch. The methods given may be worked on right or wrong side.

EDGES TO BE CONNECTED. To whip over a folded edge with a fine matching thread gives a light finish. Afterwards the surplus turning is cut away.

Loosely woven materials should have this whipped edge folded in before veining. Further strength is added by whipping a second time.

PUNCHING STITCHES. For seams, joins, outlining and appliqué.

These are open work stitches similar in effect to hem-stitching. They are formed by piercing holes with a coarse needle—No. 1 or 2 sharp. A fine sewing silk should be used so that the holes will be clear.

The stitches may be worked in any direction in contrast to hem-stitching which must follow a straight thread.

APPLIQUÉ HEM-STITCH. Commence at the right-hand side. The end of silk is left loose on the wrong side, to be afterwards darned in with a fine needle. Make a back-stitch pointing the needle to the left. A second back-stitch is taken from the same position, but diagonally. The point of the needle should emerge just above the first hole formed. The needle is now passed into the hole underneath and a straight forward stitch taken. Repeat as

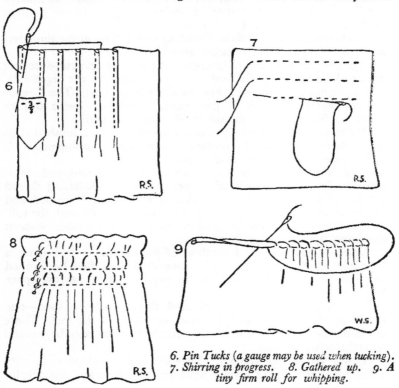

6. Pin Tucks (a gauge may be used when tucking).
7. Shirring in progress.   8. Gathered up.   9. A tiny firm roll for whipping.

from the beginning. The thread should be pulled tightly after each stitch. Size of stitch about one-tenth inch.

POINT TURC. Known also as Pin-stitch and Three-sided-stitch. It is composed of two rows of back-stitching, worked alternately above and below. The holes of one row are opposite the spaces of the other, thus forming a triangle. Size of stitch about one-tenth inch.

SEAMS THAT ARE INCONSPICUOUS. Tack carefully and freely. The finished result will justify the extra time entailed.

French Seam. Place the edges together, right sides outside. The fixing should be done flat on the table. Machine or run-stitch

6

⅛-inch from the edges. Press open the seam with a warm iron. Turn to the wrong side. Tack, and machine or run-stitch ⅛-inch from the fold.

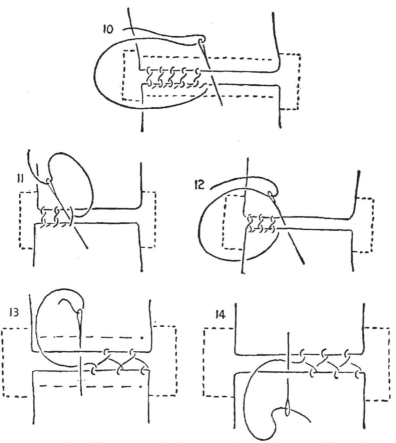

10, 11 and 12. Three stages of veining. 13 and 14. Two stages of faggoting.

Whipped Seam. A light finish for short seams in fine materials. The turning allowance is machined on to the wrong side. One edge is cut to within ⅛-inch from the stitching. The other edge is trimmed to the same amount above the first and whipped over the inner edge to make neat.

For fabric that frays easily, the outer edge should be sufficiently broad to roll on top of the inner edge before whipping.

AN OPENING. A NECESSITY. If underwear is to be in agreement with Dress it must be made to mould the figure, yet be easy and

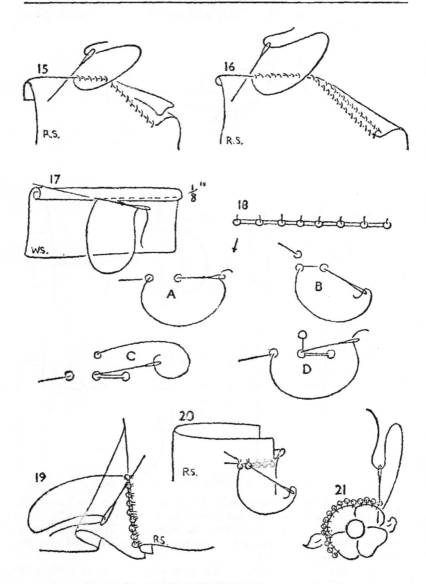

15. *Whipped edges.* 16. *Double whipping for fraying material.* 17. *Narrow runstitched hem makes strong finish for edges to be " linked."* 18. *Punching-stitch and details of same* (A B C D). 19. *Godet let into a seam by means of appliqué hemstitch.* 20. *Dart appliqué hem-stitched.* 21. *Used to appliqué a design.*

comfortable to wear. Close fit can only be achieved by the use of an opening.

Openings may occur in a seam or be cut into the material of the garment. Women's garments usually fasten right over left.

Continuous Opening. Different methods are used according to the purpose and position of an opening, but none is more adaptable than the " Continuous," where flat, invisible treatment is essential.

Length. Depends upon position, but it must be sufficiently long to allow of slipping the garment on and off easily. If a seam is to be utilised, the lay or turning on the wrong side must be

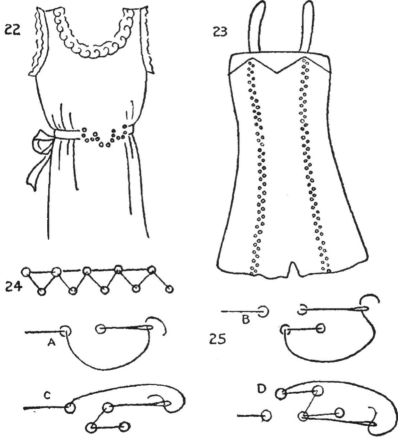

Application of Point Turc. 22. Giving bodice effect. 23. Panel effect. 24. Detail of stitch. 25. A B C D Method of Working.

snipped where the opening is to end, to allow the false piece to set flatly. If the Opening is cut into the material, the end should be strengthened with a few button-hole-stitches.

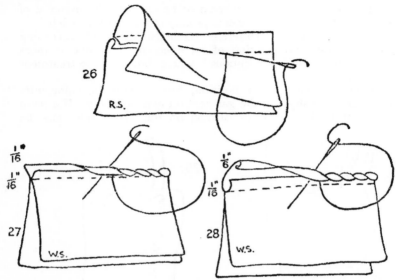

26. French seam. 27. Raw edge whipping. 28. Rolled-edge whipping when material frays.

The False Piece. This is cut selvedgewise—twice the length of the opening and fully $\frac{1}{2}$-inch to obviate any discrepancy at the top of the opening. The width is twice the finished width plus turnings. A usual finished width is $\frac{5}{8}$-inch as it allows space for working buttonholes.

To Manipulate. Place the continuous strip to the edge of the opening, right sides together. Fix, with the garment held towards the worker. On no account must the strip be eased, otherwise the opening will be neither flat nor invisible. On a cut opening the smallest possible turning should be taken from the garment at the corner. Elsewhere the machined seam should be $\frac{1}{8}$-inch.

Fold the continuous strip on to the wrong side. Turn in the free edge, and tack just above the machining. Only the portion to project as a wrap is hemmed.

Upper Edge. Cut away half the width of the false piece, the remainder is fixed flat to the garment and hemmed or machined. Make the end neat and strong with a row of hand or machine-stitching.

For a short opening where absolute flatness is not first consideration, the continuous strip may be retained intact and merely folded under against the upper edge of opening. The under portion projects as before to form a wrap. Usually the finished width of false piece is narrower (about ⅜-inch) for this arrangement of the continuous opening. No machining shows on the right side.

Decorative Openings. None is more simple than a Bound Opening or has more possibilities. Single crossway binding (see " Binding ") in matching or contrasting colour should be used.

For method of working, see Article on Openings, in the chapter on Dressmaking.

Faced Opening. Effective both as an opening and a trimming, with the advantage of easy manipulation.

Method. Cut a warp-way strip of contrasting material. Crease to define the centre. Place right side down on the wrong side over the position for the opening. Machine-stitch close, tapering to a point at the end. Cut between the two rows of machining, and turn the added strip through to the right side. The free edges are turned in and secured decoratively.

When matching material is used the process may be reversed. The added piece being turned through to the wrong side.

WAYS WITH EDGES

APPLIQUÉD LACE. The needle-run make of lace is most suitable for this modern method of dealing with lace edging and en-crustations. The pattern should be clearly defined, so that it can be followed for an edging or border, and in the case of motifs, small complete designs selected for cutting out.

If cost is a consideration, Nottingham lace should be bought in preference to machine needle-run lace which is too heavy for lingerie.

The needle-run or Nottingham lace should have surplus net and unwanted patterns cut away before application to the garment, but care must be taken not to cut the fine outlining cord.

Fix the lace in position when cut, right side uppermost. In the case of a neckline, to have a figure stand is a great advantage in arranging the lace firmly and in good line on the garment.

Joins should be matched by a pattern, overlapped, and whipped round before the attachment of the lace. One thread of stranded cotton, filoselle or sewing silk matching the lace should be used. The outer edge of lace is held towards the worker. The inner edge is whipped from right to left, following the selected pattern. Afterwards the surplus material is cut away on the wrong side, following the irregular outline of the whipping. A second line of whipping may be necessary if the lace is fragile or the material fraying badly.

One of the punching-stitches used to attach lace is particularly appropriate for its delicate task.

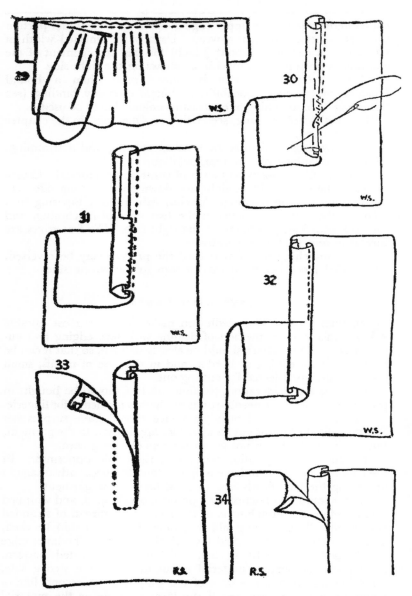

29. *Fixing the continuous strip with opening straightened out.* 30. *Folded into position.* 31. *Half the width of portion for upper edge cut away.* 32 *Upper edge fixed.* 33. *Finished appearance on right side.* 34. *Concealed opening.* (*See also Diagram of first method.*)

FRENCH STEMMING. A beautiful medium in attaching lace, net borders and insets, which cannot be overlooked. Embroidery silk matching either the material or lace should be used—one or two strands of filoselle or stranded cotton is most satisfactory in giving a fine line. The stitch, which may be padded, is worked on the right side from left to right with the work held flatly over the first finger of the left hand. If the material is folded as for top-sewing, the edge is more liable to stretch in working. The surplus material is afterwards cut away on the wrong side.

LACE AND NET EDGING. Tiny frills of lace and picot-edged net are delightfully dainty and most simple to achieve. Lingerie lace with a net ground has a thread woven into the edge which will " draw up." Ready frilled lace and net can also be bought by the yard.

The edging should be gathered and, as for previous methods, joined into a circle if necessary before application. A counter-hem seam is the best means of joining picot-edged net since there is no design to match and overlap. One of the punching-stitches or French stemming may be chosen as the medium of attachment.

NET APPLIQUÉ. The term appliqué is used in embroidery to signify a form of decoration in which one kind of material is applied upon another to form a pattern. In net appliqué it is the garment edge usually which is imposed on the net. A fine Brussels net is most durable and washes splendidly. As only a small quantity is required —⅛ or ¼-yard according to purpose—the cost will be less than buying lace edging. Georgette may be used in place of the net.

The design, which should be clear and simple in outline, is lightly traced on to the garment by means of carbon paper. Double net is then tacked on behind to extend beyond the pattern. If the edge is straight, the folded edge of net may be retained as the finished edge of garment. But where the outline is irregular, the net edge must be bound, or otherwise made neat. French stemming, loop-stitch or one of the punching stitches may be used to outline the design. In each case working through material and net.

A padding of run-stitching is a necessary preliminary to the first two methods. Embroidery thread as recommended for stemming is used. When the embroidery is complete the surplus material is cut away on the right side, also surplus net on the wrong side. Details such as stalks, leaves and tendrils, too small to appliqué, may be embroidered in satin or stem-stitch.

PICOT-EDGING. French stemming is again requisitioned and combined with bullions to give an exquisite edge. If the material is on the bias, run-stitch as a preliminary will prevent stretching. The turning is then folded to the wrong side by the line of run-stitching, and stemming worked over the folded edge from right

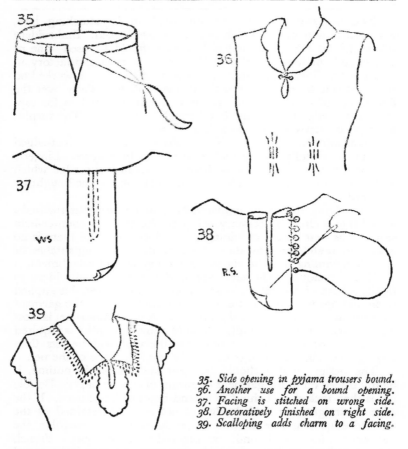

35. *Side opening in pyjama trousers bound.*
36. *Another use for a bound opening.*
37. *Facing is stitched on wrong side.*
38. *Decoratively finished on right side.*
39. *Scalloping adds charm to a facing.*

to left, with a break at regular intervals of bullion stitches. To work bullion-stitch the thread as it emerges is wound several times round the point of the needle. The twists should be held lightly in position with the left thumb until the needle is pulled through. When the next stem-stitch is worked the bullion-stitch rolls into position over the edge. Afterwards the surplus material is cut away on the wrong side.

SCALLOPING

L OOP-STITCH worked closely on an edge that is to be cut out, gives that individual note which is only possible with hand work.

Though transfers in various sizes and designs may be bought, the self-made pattern which can be drawn to fit a given outline is more accurate and satisfactory in every way.

THE DESIGN. Two parallel lines, not more than $\frac{1}{8}$-inch apart for fine work, should be ruled or curved on paper. A small button or a threepenny piece is used to define the scallop. Only the tip of the disc should be outlined, otherwise the scallops will lose much of their beauty and be more difficult to embroider. The entire area need not be drawn, but planned so that the junction of two

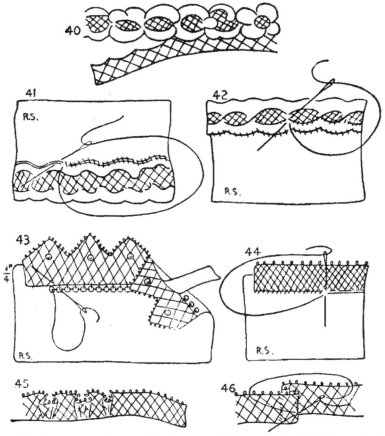

40. *Cutting away surplus net from lace.* 41. *The outer edge is held towards the worker.* 42. *Two rows of whipping for fraying material.* 43. *Lace edging with appliqué hem-stitch. (Surplus material on wrong side is cut away.)* 44. *French stemming—stitches worked close together will give a lustrous line.* 45. *Frilled edging.* 46. *How to join net edge.*

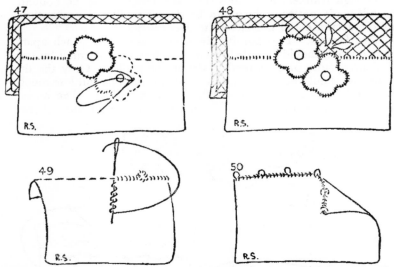

Net appliqué. 47. Stemming the design. 48. Surplus material is cut away on right side. Picot edging. 49. Twisting the thread for a bullion-stitch. 50. Picots at intervals of ¼ to ⅜-inch.

scallops or a complete pattern falls at the centre of the garment. corners require special treatment. Where the edge is straightforward a template of two or three scallops is adequate, and can be readily adapted to fit in.

The design may be lightly traced directly on to the garment, using a sharp blue pencil to follow the scalloped edge of the template.

Another method is to place a small piece of carbon paper between the template—the scalloped edge of which is not cut out—and the garment, before the tracing operation. A knitting needle is then used to follow the outline. Pins should never be passed through carbon paper to the material or an unwanted mark will result. Only the paper pattern should be pinned to the garment, and the small piece of coloured carbon slipped underneath.

How to Work. Use fine embroidery silk or cotton previously recommended. Pad by run-stitching the scallops, inserting the needle at each corner. The loop-stitch is worked closely over the run-stitches with the knotted edge to the outside. Straight stitches, with one upright at each corner, may be used, or they may radiate from the centre of each scallop. Afterwards the surplus material edge is cut away.

Faced Scalloping. An excellent finish for a lower edge, or where a heavier treatment is no disadvantage.

A facing of self material is cut to correspond in shape with the edge of the garment. Allowance must be made for the depth of the scallops, also a hem if required, and turnings. Fix the false piece into position right sides together, centres and seams matching.

Plan the number of scallops necessary for the given length. These may be drawn on paper to the required size with two parallel lines to act as guide, or outline less than half round a large coin, cup or saucer. The former is the better and more accurate method.

Trace the pattern on to the facing, using one of the methods described under " Scalloping."

Machine-stitch round the scalloped outline, through facing and garment. The surplus material beyond the scallops is cut away to ⅛-inch from the machining. Each corner must be snipped to allow the facing to be turned on to the wrong side. Pull each scallop into shape, tack and press. Fold in the free edge and machine-stitch or lightly hem.

BINDING. One of the indispensable processes in needlework. Strong, yet dainty and most accommodating. It may be adapted equally well to straight, curved or irregular outlines, and without added cost, since cuttings of material may be utilised. Where edges are to be inconspicuously treated, binding is usually the best method to employ. Carried out in different material, a contrasting colour, or a deeper tone of the garment hue, it makes an attractive trimming.

PREPARING THE BINDING. Unless a contrast is required, and there are no cuttings available, bought bias binding is not advocated in Lingerie. If it is necessary in order to get a certain colour note, the quality should be good, and the width reduced by cutting.

The first essential in achieving a beautifully neat, smooth bind is to have the strips cut on the exact cross of the fabric, otherwise they will most certainly twist in manipulation. The edges must be cleanly cut and the strips of equal width. Therefore cut each strip from single material after careful measurement. Joins must run true to the warp grain if they are to be inconspicuous and strong.

SINGLE OR DOUBLE STRIPS may be used. For fabrics of fine texture, the latter will give a firmer, neater edge, while for heavier materials the single method is not so bulky. To calculate for single binding allow twice the finished breadth plus turnings (usually ⅛-inch). For double binding allow four times the finished breadth plus turnings (usually ¾-inch).

APPLICATION. *Single Binding*. Fix right sides together and machine-stitch the strip to the garment with ⅛-inch seam. Roll the binding on to the wrong side. Fold in the free edge to meet the raw edges of the seam, and lightly hem just above the machining.

DOUBLE BINDING. Fold the strips double, baste, and if of silk

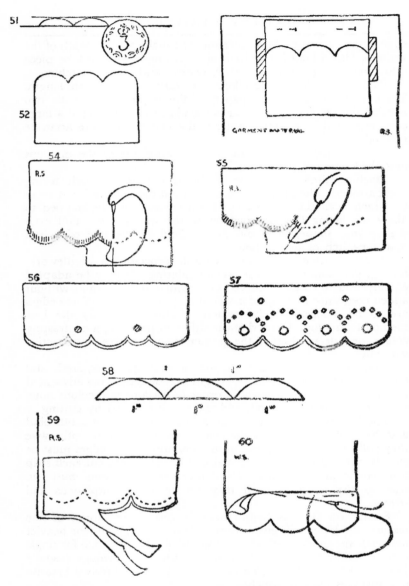

51. Use of a coin in scallop design. 52. Template cut ready for use. 53. Uncut template with carbon paper. 54. Scalloped with straight stitches. 55. Stitches radiating from the centre make corners appear to overlap. 56. Composite scallops are interesting. 57. Possibilities with scalloping. 58. Method of drawing large scallops. 59. Prepare the edges before turning out the scallops. 60. The free edge is folded in on the W.S.

press lightly. Place to the right side of the edge to be bound, and machine ⅛-inch in. Roll the bind on to the wrong side. Hem the fold lightly above the machining.

CURVES IN BINDING. These require careful manipulation. When applying to an outer curve, such as a scallop or a lower edge, the binding should be eased to prevent contraction. On an inner curve—neckline or armline—the reverse is the case, the binding must be slightly strained to prevent stretching.

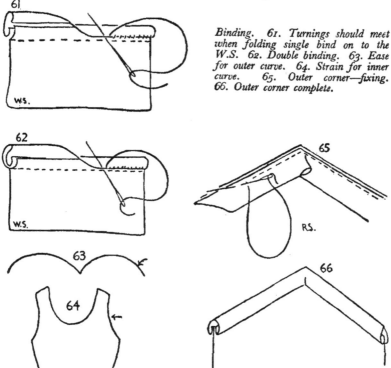

Binding. 61. Turnings should meet when folding single bind on to the W.S. 62. Double binding. 63. Ease for outer curve. 64. Strain for inner curve. 65. Outer corner—fixing. 66. Outer corner complete.

CORNERS IN BINDING. These also present difficulties. An outside corner must be turned by means of a small pleat. To turn an inside corner, the garment turning should first be snipped to allow the edge to straighten out for easier manipulation. The binding strip is strained at the corner also, and when finished mitred. Where the indentation is indefinite, as in shallow scallops, it is not possible to mitre.

SHELL-EDGE BINDING. This is an interesting development which makes an effective trimming, either in self or contrasting

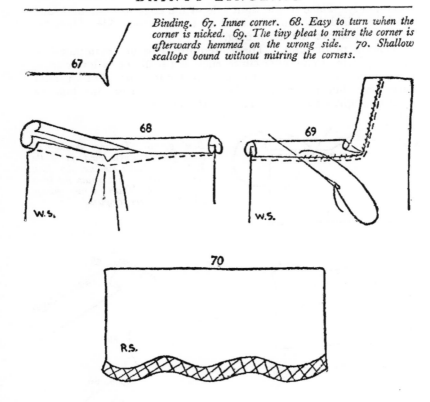

Binding. 67. Inner corner. 68. Easy to turn when the corner is nicked. 69. The tiny pleat to mitre the corner is afterwards hemmed on the wrong side. 70. Shallow scallops bound without mitring the corners.

colour. White, shell-edged with thread matching the colour of the garment, is a pleasing combination.

To Work. Proceed to bind the edge with single binding. The shell-edging is formed simultaneously with the hemming on the wrong side, by working a double over-cast stitch at intervals of ¼-inch. One strand of filoselle or stranded cotton should be used.

SHELL-EDGING. This gives the garment directly a similar effect, but lighter and not so strong. It provides an excellent finish for the edges of frills and draperies.

To Work. A narrow hem of ⅛-inch is tacked on to the wrong side. The edge of the hem is merely " whipped " with the hemming stitches, so that only the over-casting stitches indenting the edge show on the right side.

ROULEAUX. This is a development of binding on more decorative lines. The veined or faggot-stitched attachment gives quite an exclusive air.

To Prepare. The Rouleaux, cut on the cross and very narrow (½-inch wide) may be prepared in two ways.

(1). Turn the edges in to meet in the centre. Fold double and tack.

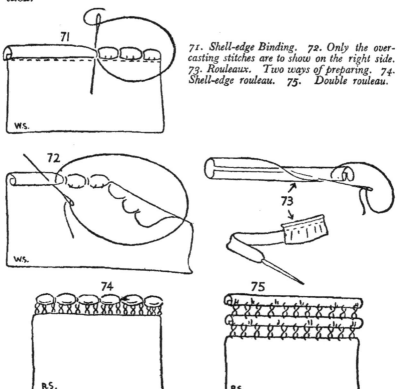

71. *Shell-edge Binding.* 72. *Only the overcasting stitches are to show on the right side.* 73. *Rouleaux. Two ways of preparing.* 74. *Shell-edge rouleau.* 75. *Double rouleau.*

(2). Fold double and run-stitch close to the edges on the wrong side. Sew one end temporarily to a wool needle and pull through to the right side. Press very lightly—seam to edge—as the name implies Rouleaux should be rounded, not flat. (See " Veining " for method of attachment.)

DECORATION

THE scheme of decoration that is most satisfying and pleasing is the one planned with the conception of the garment, and incorporated in its construction, as indicated in decorative treatment of seams and fulness, with beautifully finished edges. It may be, however, that a purely ornamental addition is a necessary enrichment to unify the whole, and it is just here that the inexperienced may go astray.

With the use of silk for under-garments there has been a corresponding change in the form of decoration. What was appropriate for linen and cotton has been found too ornate for rich materials, which require little if any further embellishment.

Points to Consider. 1. Any form of decoration should be chosen with a view to showing the material to best advantage—not because of the beauty of the embroidery itself.

2. It should appear as if it were part of the material, and be in agreement with the other finishes, not divorced from them.

3. Also, it must be suited to the purpose of the garment.

So simple are the designs used for lingerie decoration, that with a little ingenuity they may be easily evolved without any special knowledge of design.

Repetition of simple shapes is one of the first principles to follow. Take a circle or dot and leaf form for example :

The Circle. This is also a very important unit for conventional floral designs. Naturalistic flower forms are unsuitable as lingerie decoration. They also require expert technique.

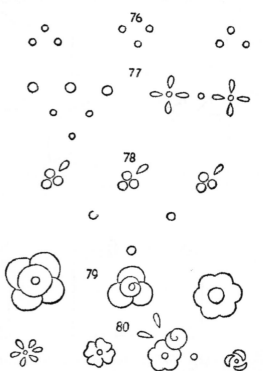

76, 77, 78. Repetition of simple shapes to form pattern for lingerie decoration. 79 and 80. Circle and leaf forms.

The designs should be built up on paper first, with the selected motifs cut out, so that they may be moved about, and outlined when an harmonious arrangement is reached. The method of transferring a design is described under " Scalloping."

Geometrical Forms. Designs can be readily worked out on

squared paper. They are appropriate especially for drawn thread work and shadow embroidery.

The treatment of stitchery must be considered when planning designs, and the units selected accordingly. Ideas for motifs, and inspiration for their execution can be got from Period and typical examples of embroidery, their illustrations, the flower and leaf forms in laces, and many other sources.

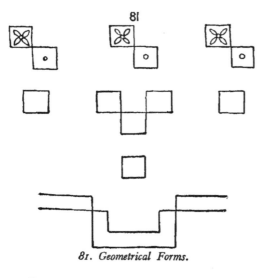

81. *Geometrical Forms.*

Colour is an important factor. Pastel tones and self colour in harmony with the background material and in keeping with the design are a right choice. Charming effects may be got by repeating in the embroidery the colour note of the edges.

For the execution of any design to be applied, the reader is advised to turn to the Chapter on "Embroidery." Several stitches described earlier in this article can be applied in purely decorative fashion—punching stitches and French stemming for appliqué, outlining, stems and tendrils, also for initials and monograms. Eyelets are worked by means of French stemming after being pierced with a stiletto, or cut. Satin-stitch is simply stemming in broader form and more heavily padded. Loop-stitch is also used for appliqué and Richelieu work. Bullion-stitch as described under "Picot-Edging" is a favourite and very expeditious medium for small sprays and all over patterns.

KNICKER TYPE

THIRD TYPE

KNICKERS (For children and girls, 2 or 3 years to 12 years.)

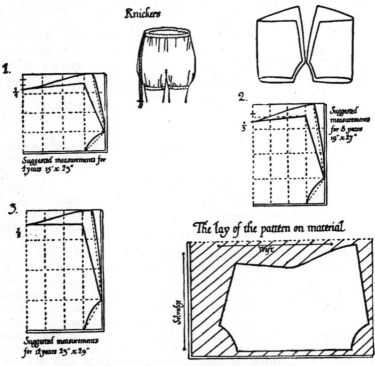

Knickers

1.

$\frac{1}{4}$

Suggested measurements for 4 years 15" x 23"

2.

$\frac{1}{4}$

$\frac{1}{3}$

Suggested measurements for 8 years 19" x 27"

3.

$\frac{1}{4}$

Suggested measurements for 12 years 23" x 29"

The lay of the pattern on material

Width

Selvedge

KNICKERS (For girls, 2 or 3 years to 12 years.)

Measurements Required.

Side waist to knee for length, the widths vary for different ages. These patterns are made to the knee. Measure up from the knee to the required position and cut away the amount from the leg of the pattern.

1. 2 or 3 years to 5 years.

Length is side length + 2 ins.
Width is 1½ times length. Fold this in half along selvedge.
Folds. 4 each way.
Leg. 1 division each way.
Back waist. ½ division in.
Side waist. ¾ division down.
Front waist. 1 division in and ½ division down.

2. 5 or 6 years to 10 years.

Length is side length + 2 ins. to 3 ins.
Width is 1⅓ times length. Fold this in half along selvedge.
Folds. 4 each way.
Leg. 1 division each way.
Back waist. ½ division in.
Side waist. ⅔ division down.
Front waist. 1 division in and ½ division down.

3. 10 to 12 years.

Length is side length + 3 ins. to 4 ins.
Width is 1¼ length. Fold this in half along selvedge.
Folds. 4 each way.
Leg. 1 division each way.
Back waist. ½ division in.
Side waist. ½ division down.
Front waist. 1 division in and ¼ division down.

To cut out. (Keep paper folded, with fold on left.)

Cut out the outer pattern lines on the double paper. Lift the top paper and cut front waist and centre front line to the fork.

The Lay of the Pattern on the Material.

Fold the material along the weft with the wrong or right sides facing. Place the pattern with the knee to the cut edges and the back towards the selvedge.

KNICKERS (For adults.)

Knickers for adults

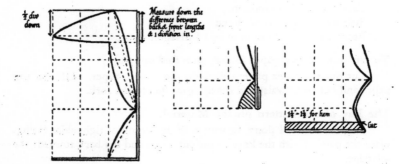

½ div down

Measure down the difference between back & front lengths & 1 division in.

1¼ - 1½ for hem

Cut

KNICKERS (For adults.)

Measurements Necessary.

More measurements are required than in the case of children, owing to greater variation in build and a closer fit being required. The back length in sitting posture is taken, because of the great difference in measurements between the erect and sitting postures. This difference varies considerably on different figures.

1. Hip measurement taken 7 ins. to 8 ins. below the waist.
2. Back length taken in sitting posture from half way between the centre back and side at the waist to the knee.
3. Front length from waist to the knee.

Size of Paper Pattern.

Length. Back length taken in a sitting posture.
Width. ¾ hip measure + 2 ins. to 3 ins. Fold paper in half lengthways. Fold into thirds both ways.

Back.

Leg. 1 division each way.
Back waist. ¾ or 1 division in.
Side waist. ½ division down.
Front waist. Measure down on the right the difference between front length and back length and 1 division in.
Centre back line. Curve slightly outwards.
Centre front line. Curve inwards.

This pattern reaches the knee which is not a fashionable length. Measure up from the knee the length at which the garment is required and fold the pattern back at this length. If this is done before cutting out the pattern an allowance about 1¼ ins. to 1½ ins. may be made for the hem at the knee. This would turn back and fit over the leg seam.

Before cutting the pattern, the waist line may be tested for size. It should be ½ hip + 2 ins.

FRONT

Neck: 1½ division in and 2 divisions down from *A*.

Shoulder as back.

Width at bust = ¼ bust + 1 in. and 1 in. below bust line.

Yoke line 2 in. below armhole. Drop 1 in. to 1½ in. in front and spring ¾ in. for bust accommodation.

For the *bodice* extend the side line to the waist and the centre front to 1 in. below. Take out a small dart midway between front and seam.

Omit the spring in front and reduce the waist ½ in. at the underarm.

The *skirt* is formed of two straight widths of material cut to the required length plus hem. These are each gored to measure ½ hip + 3 in. at 8 in. down.

For the *sleeve* use a seam-to-seam pattern (Fig. 22), with *depth of sleeve head, AB, only* ¼ *armhole* to balance the long shoulder of nightgown.

Make the total length 1 in. less than measurement for the same reason.

For a *puffed* sleeve decrease the shoulder width in preference to shortening the sleeve head. The extra length that forms the "puff" of a nightgown's sleeves is allowed equally at head and at the lower edge of sleeve.

WOMAN'S KNICKERS

By paper folding. Turnings allowed in pattern.

MEASUREMENTS

Side length from waist to ground when kneeling .	.	26 in.
Hip measure 8 in. below waist	.	40 in.

DIMENSIONS OF PAPER

Length = side length + 4 in. or ⅜ height + 2 in. .	.	30 in.
Width = ¾ hip measure	.	30 in.

Fold paper in half lengthwise, then into 3 each way.

Open to half and place fold to left. Mark *ABCD* (Fig. 34).

Directoire Knickers

PATTERN FOR DIRECTOIRE KNICKERS

Waist. Side = 4 in. below *B*. Dot horizontal line to right.

Front = ⅛ width in from *A* and 1 in. lower than side.

Back = ¼ width in from *A*.

Leg. DE = ⅓ *AD*.

Knee = ⅔ width from *C*. Curve sharply from *E*, keeping the line straight above the knee.

Front seam. Dot a guiding line from front waist to the fork *E* and divide into thirds. Mark 1½ in. in at ⅓ above *E*.

Draw front seam straight from the waist, curving through this point to *E*.

Back seam. Test the size of waist and add, if necessary, at the back to make it equal ½ hip + 2 in. for knickers drawn up with elastic.

Draw in the back seam by a slightly curved line from waist to fork.
This pattern fits to the knee and would be too long for present wear.
Reduce the length of leg by half a division (or as desired) and add $1\frac{1}{4}$ in.
for hem (Fig. 34, dotted line).

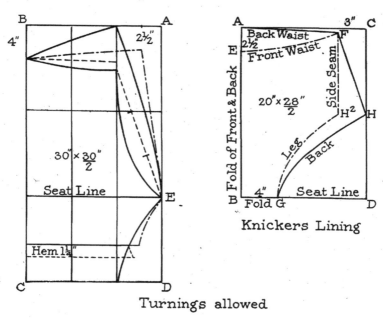

Turnings allowed

Fig. 34

WOMAN'S KNICKERS

Fig. 35

French Knickers

For *French knickers* with open-fitting knee line—
Make the *length of leg* = $\frac{1}{2}$ DE.
Make *width at knee* = $2\frac{1}{2}$ divisions. Add for hem if required.
At the *waist* reduce the dip between front and back by half, because the loose-fitting knee makes the garment hang like a skirt.
Thus the back waist is lowered $2\frac{1}{2}$ in. and the width increased by $\frac{1}{2}$ division. Rule the back seam to E (Fig. 34, dot and dash line). See also Fig. 36 (*c*)).

29

Knickers Lining

These may be cut from the knicker pattern by shortening the leg 1 in. and finishing with a narrow hem.

Or a separate pattern may be used as Fig. 35, with fold at centre back and front, a weft fold on the seat line and seams at the side.

Length = length of knicker pattern to seat (AE of Fig. 34) = 20 in.

Width = $\frac{3}{4}$ of hip measure – 2 in. (28 in.).

AB = length (20 in.). AC = half width (14 in.).

Rule rectangle $ABDC$.

Waist line. Front, AE = $2\frac{1}{2}$ in.

              Side, CF = 3 in. in and $\frac{1}{2}$ in. down. Curve FE for the front and draw in the back waist AF.

                    BG = 4 in.

Leg. DH = $\frac{1}{4}$ CD. Curve for H to G for the back. For front, HH^2 = 3 in.

Side seam. Rule FH and FH^2 for back and front respectively, and make the two equal in length.

Cami-knickers

Cami-knickers are a combination of camisole and knickers.

The garment may be cut from either the princess petticoat foundation (Fig. 36 (a)), or from the petticoat bodice and French knicker pattern (with slightly wider waist (Fig 36 (b, c)).

Only the plain patterns are given below, decorative seam lines would be added as desired.

MEASUREMENTS—AVERAGE SIZE

Bust	.	. . .	. 36 in.	Underarm . . . 8 in.
Waist	.	. .	. 30 in.	Length below waist . 18 in. to 20 in.
Hips	.	. .	. 40 in.	

I. CAMI-KNICKERS IN ONE PIECE
The Bodice

AB. Bust line = $\frac{1}{4}$ bust.

AC = underarm measurement. Complete the rectangle.

For the "Brassière top" measure $3\frac{1}{2}$ in. to left from A and 3 in. up, rule from this point to A and curve to B.

Waist line: Reduce the width 1 in. at the side (D); the back waist is straight to C, and the front curved to C^2 $1\frac{1}{2}$ in. below C. Rule from B to D for the side seam.

The Knicker

C^2E = 8 in., draw the hip line at this level to equal $\frac{1}{4}$ hip measurement + $\frac{1}{2}$ in.

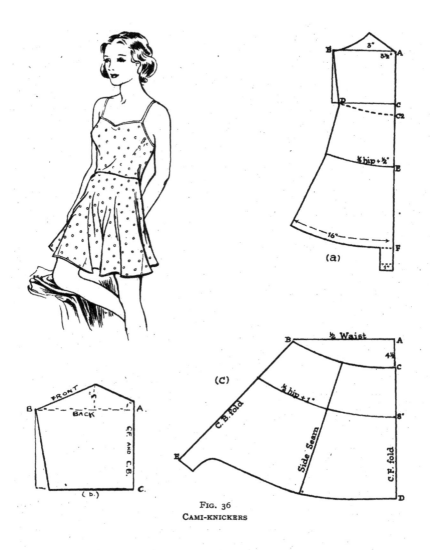

FIG. 36
CAMI-KNICKERS

C^2F = the length measurement 18 in. to 20 in. This is the same for back and front and thus allows $1\frac{1}{2}$ in. further length for bend to the back.

Width at leg = 16 in. Rule the side seam from D through the hip line to equal C^2F at the required width.

The Strap. This is added to the back to be $3\frac{3}{4}$ in. finished including $\frac{3}{4}$ in. overlap, the width (on pattern) is 3 in.

For *shoulder straps* allow $\frac{7}{8}$ yd. of washing ribbon $\frac{3}{8}$ in. wide.

II. CAMI-KNICKERS WITH WAIST SEAM
The Bodice

This is similar to the previous pattern but with an "Opera top" and bust accommodation allowed on upper instead of lower edge of bodice (Fig. 36 (*b*)).

$AB = \frac{1}{4}$ bust. AC = underarm measurement, draw in the rectangle.

For the "opera top" raise the line 1 in. at the centre front, thus giving the effect of a dart at the underarm; keep the line horizontal for 2 in. from centre front and side, and curve the remainder or shape as in diagram.

Waist Line. Reduce the width 1 in. at the side and keep the line straight for front and back.

The Knicker

$AB = \frac{1}{2}$ waist measurement.

$AC = 4\frac{1}{2}$ in. Draw in the waist curve keeping the line almost straight towards the back.

Hip line. 8 in. below the waist = $\frac{1}{2}$ hip + 1 in.

Length. Front CD = the length measurement 18 in. to 20 in.

Side = $CD + 1$ ruled through the middle of waist and hip lines.

Back. BE = $CD + 4$ in. Make strap 3 in. wide and complete as in diagram.

NOTE. 1. Both the above patterns are close-fitting and will require an opening at the side. If desired wider, the bust line (AB) may be taken as $\frac{1}{4}$ bust $+ \frac{1}{2}$ in. and only $\frac{1}{2}$ in. suppression at the side waist (D). The waist line (AB) of knicker (Fig. 36 (*c*)) would then be taken as $\frac{1}{2}$ *waist measurement of bodice*—1 in.

2. When cutting out pattern (*a*) place centre back and front to the fold joined by the strap piece; or if preferred the back and front may be cut separately and the strap buttoned on to the front.

The knicker pattern (*C*) may be cut with centre front and back on the direct cross of the material, or to the warp fold as desired.

French Knickers

This popular type of knickers is cut similar to the lower portion of the above garment (Fig. 36 (*c*)), but AB would be made $\frac{1}{2}$ waist—$1\frac{1}{2}$ in. to make the knickers close fitting.

MAKING YOUR UNDERWEAR

ONCE you have made frocks, you will find underwear a very simple task. Except for certain nightwear, there are no collars and sleeves to be made, and the dainty garments are finished before one has time to tire. By making underwear at home one can have lovely hand-worked lingerie which would cost fabulous prices if bought ready-made; better still, these garments lend themselves to such delicate materials and such exquisite stitchery that they are really enchanting to make.

So if you love embroidery and beautiful workmanship you will take naturally to lingerie-making. It is specially suitable, too, for the woman without a sewing machine. It is no good making a fetish of hand sewing, of course, if you have a machine, for it saves a good deal of time; but the fact remains that the finest undies are sewn entirely by hand.

You will want one or two extra tools, in addition to the equipment given on pages 6–7; but these cost only a small sum. The first is an emery pincushion which prevents needles from rusting. This can be bought from most haberdashery counters, and is very necessary, for a rusty needle can easily leave an ugly mark on fine fabrics.

You will also need a stiletto, for piercing the holes when working eyelets or *broderie anglaise*, and a pair of small, sharp embroidery scissors.

Very fine needles and cottons are essential if you are to make the really tiny stitches that go into good lingerie. So put away your No. 40 cottons and No. 7 needles. Get instead No. 80 cotton and Nos. 8 and 9 needles, and your fairylike stitches will delight you! Silk, and silk substitute threads, are not graded as closely as cottons, and you will sometimes have to use these. But on many pale materials stitches are less visible if made in really fine white cotton than in a coarser matching thread.

Now for one or two items that will keep your work spotless while you are making it. This isn't just fuss, please, for half the charm of good underwear lies in its gossamer freshness. It is difficult to believe that the best lingerie in the best shops was ever patiently sewn together; one would say that fairies, rather than human hands, had made it!

Tiny stitchery is part of the secret; the rest lies in meticulous care in handling the work. So, please, provide yourself with a light-coloured washable apron with a bib to wear during lingerie-making, and keep the work, between

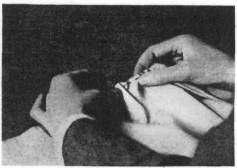

Fig. 58. The position of the hands when doing turkey-stitch. The eye of the needle is pressed against the side of the thimble

sewing times, wrapped in white tissue paper in a dustproof box or suitcase.

And, PLEASE (this is *so* important!), always wash your hands just before starting to sew, even if they look perfectly clean.

Now for stitches. You will not use a great many for the plain sewing part of the work, and most of these are ordinary dressmaking stitches, such as the French seam (almost always used for modern underwear), running, overcasting, slipstitching, and whipping.

But very likely you do not know one very useful lingerie stitch. It is really ordinary running stitch done in a quicker way, and is known as French running or turkey-stitch.

Fig. 58 shows how it is done. The chief trick to acquire

is to get your hold of material and needle right; the rest is practice.

The hold is the same with both hands—first fingers behind the work, thumbs in front. This stitch is a very quick one because, once the needle is inserted, it is not drawn out again until the seam or gathering is done. Paris seamstresses French-run almost like lightning.

Holding the work as described, with the right hand insert the needle and take up two or three stitches. In ordinary running the needle bobs in and out of the stuff, but in French running you keep the needle still, its eye pressed against your thimble, as in the photograph, to steady it, while your left hand urges the stuff on to the needle in little rucks that form stitches.

When the needle is full of stitches, work them off on to the cotton, but do not draw out the needle. Instead, urge another group of stitches on to it with the left hand, and pass them off on to the cotton in their turn. Only at the end of the line pull the needle out and regulate the row of stitches.

When you first try this stitch it seems far from being a lightning one, owing to the unfamiliar hold. But practice makes perfect—and saves such a lot of time! Sew all your gathers and French seams with turkey-stitch when making hand-sewn underwear.

In general, you will find that the sewing rules and methods described for frocks apply also to the making of "underneaths," provided you always bear in mind when choosing stitches or finishes that the main points to consider in lingerie are daintiness and ability to stand constant laundering. However, there are just a few special jobs in this kind of dressmaking which are not needed for frock-making.

For instance, you need to know how to handle such things as shoulder-straps, casings and gussets.

Shoulder-straps play an important part in underwear. From them hang many garments, such as slips and cami-bockers, and they are often partly visible through thin dresses. It is very important that they should be strong, neat and dainty, and firmly attached to the garment.

The narrower the straps, the more expensive and charming they look. Narrow ones are a little more fiddling to make, however, so an inexperienced needlewoman should start with those of medium width. Straps from $\frac{1}{4}$ in. to $\frac{1}{2}$ in. wide when finished look nice on almost any undergarments. They may be of ribbon or self-material, double satin ribbon being most durable when ribbon is used. But, in most cases, self-material is cheaper and washes and wears better.

Cut shoulder-straps twice the width they are to be, plus $\frac{1}{2}$ in. for turnings, and long enough to reach the *bottom* of the hem or lace edge which finishes the top of the garment, plus 1 in. for turnings.

Fold the strip lengthwise. Seam the two long edges together with $\frac{1}{4}$ in. turnings. Turn the tube thus made right side out with a bodkin, as described for rouleaux on page 86. Press

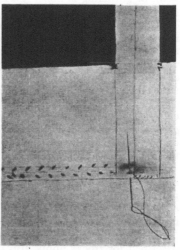

Fig. 59. Sew a shoulder-strap to a slip or cami-knickers at top and bottom only

the tube out flat into a strap, pressing so that the seam comes down the centre of one side, not along an edge (Fig. 59).

This photograph also shows the correct way of sewing the strap to the garment. Turn in each end $\frac{1}{2}$ in., and pin it to the lower edge of the bust hem, or trimming of the garment (this may be of either lace or net instead of the deep featherstitched hem illustrated). Try on the garment to test the position and length of the straps, shortening or pinning them farther in towards front or back if they show any tendency to slip.

A common fault is to pin the straps too close to the arms, making them almost certain to slide off the shoulders in wear.

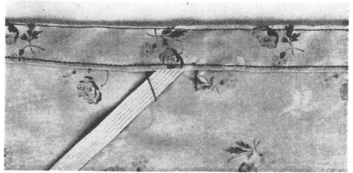

Fig. 60. The stitching between the two ends of cotton in this casing is through the fold only, so that elastic may be inserted

Usually, the best position for them is 2 in. away from the arm at the front, and $2\frac{1}{2}$ in. or 3 in. in at the back.

When adjusted comfortably, sew each strap in place at the lower edge by overcasting the folded end to the hem or lace. Then secure each side of the strap with a few neat, strong stitches to the top edge of the garment. It is very clumsy to hem a strap down on all its four sides.

Casings are much used in underwear, chiefly to hold elastics which draw up knickers at the waist, or knee, or both. On a straight edge, the casing may be the top part of the garment turned down in a hem; but on a curved edge it must be made from a bias-cut strip, or one shaped to match the curve. In either case make the casing $\frac{1}{4}$ in. wider than the elastic used. Machine along the hem, then machine again close to the folded edge (Fig. 60). This second line of stitching takes the rub of the elastic and so saves the fold of material from being worn through.

So that the elastic may be renewed easily when it perishes, without opening part of the seam, make the simple casing opening indicated by two short ends of thread and the insertion of elastic, shown in Fig. 60.

It is very easy and quick. When starting to stitch down the hem edge of the casing, for the first inch stitch only the fold, not going through the main part of the garment. Keeping the thread unbroken, fold down the casing and stitch it to the garment all round.

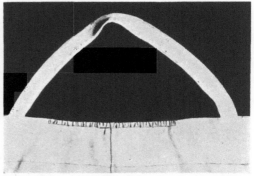

FIG. 61. An under-arm casing should occupy two-thirds of the distance from strap to strap

If a slip or cami-knickers are not to bulge under the arm, these undies should be provided with an under-arm casing fitted with elastic, as in Fig. 61. Machine a narrow casing in the top part of a wide top hem, as shown, or use that portion of the top hem itself if it is narrow.

The casing should extend only two-thirds of the distance between the front and back ends of the shoulder strap, and the elastic should draw it up about 2 in. shorter.

Gussets are small squares inserted at the junction of seams between the legs of the closed type of knickers. The gusset gives the extra play which is necessary when the garment is drawn in at the knee.

As extra strength is needed at this point, it is well to use a double gusset. Cut two squares—from 3½ in. to 4 in., plus turnings, is the usual size. Join one square to the garment with plain seams. Turn single turnings on the second square, place it over the raw edges of the first one and slipstitch it down.

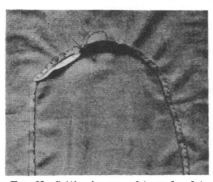

FIG. 62. Setting in a round-topped godet and overcasting nicked and plain edges together

If a single gusset is used, run-and-fell it in place. You will remember that a run-and-fell seam is a plain seam with one turning cut off very narrow, the other folded down over it, its edge turned in and hemmed down to the stuff.

Godets, usually flared, are a useful way of inserting fullness into the sides and fronts of slips, the hips of knickers or pyjama trousers. They must be carefully and neatly inset to look well. The shaped top edge of the godet may be square or pointed, or rounded as in Fig. 62.

Cut and mark the seam line of a godet very accurately. To join it to the garment, turn in singly the corresponding edges of the garment, and lap the turn over the godet edges, along the marked seam line. At corners, in the case of square or pointed godets, or at intervals of ¼ in. along rounded ones, the garment edges must be slashed to make them lie flat along the godet outline.

Slash *before* seaming—in fact, slash as you tack. After machining, press both turnings outwards. Neaten by overcasting them together, taking a separate overcasting stitch through each individual slash.

LACE-TRIMMED LINGERIE

NO trimming is more popular and more dainty for underwear than lace, and its cousin, net, is a close second. There are several ways in which these trimmings can be applied to the garments at varying speeds.

Of course, lace *can* be machined on to underwear. This is the quickest but the clumsiest way—and lingerie should never be the least bit clumsy. So do take the trouble to practise two or three of the dainty methods I am describing in this chapter, until you can do them with the sure hand and fairylike touch which turn out really exquisite garments. For photographic purposes I have had to enlarge and coarsen my stitches; but actually, of course, they should be made tiny and delicate.

Most of these methods of adding lace edgings to material are equally applicable to net edgings or hems. In the case of hems made from piece net, cut them twice the width required, plus ½ in. Double the net lengthwise, and press in single ¼-in. turnings to face each other on each thickness.

Here are five ways of joining lace edgings to underwear.

1. *Whipping* needs practice, but when well done gives beautiful results. Leave only very tiny turnings on the edge of stuff that is to be whipped.

Roll the edge inwards into a tiny fine roll that conceals the raw edge, doing this between thumb and forefinger of the left hand, while you hold the wrong side of the stuff towards you. Roll only an inch or two at a time. Then secure the roll by taking whipping or overcasting stitches over it (see the left-hand needle in Fig. 63). In some materials it is easier to roll finely and neatly if you first run a line of machine stitching just inside the raw edge and roll the edge over this.

As each portion is rolled and whipped, follow behind with a second needle and cotton, whipping the edge of the lace over the whipped hem (Fig. 63, right-hand needle). This is the easiest plan for a beginner; but when you can roll neatly you will be able

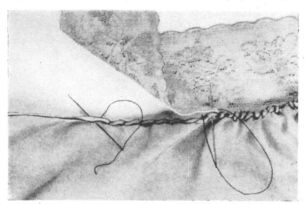

Fig. 63. Details of whipping a rolled edge (*left needle*), and whipping lace to a gathered edge (*right needle*)

to use only one needle, catching the lace in place with the same stitch that holds down the roll.

When joining lace to a gathered edge, however, whip the edge separately as in the photograph, drawing it up every few inches into the necessary gathers. Then use a second line of whipping to secure the lace to the gathered roll.

2. *Overcasting.* First-class dressmakers do not recognize this method, for it has not quite the exquisite neatness of some. But for speed and easiness it is the best of all.

Place the lace against the stuff, right sides touching, the *plain* edge of the lace running ¼ in. below the raw edge of the stuff (Fig. 64). Then overcast lace and material together with small, close stitches pulled rather tight. The overcasting crumples up

41

LACE-TRIMMED LINGERIE

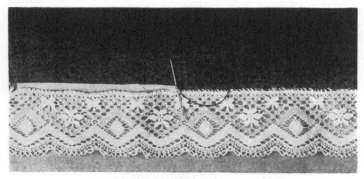

Fig. 64. Overcasting lace to a raw edge

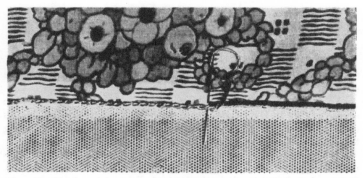

Fig. 65. Net hem joined to garment by a row of satin-stitch, first padded with chain-stitch

the raw edge of the fabric, making a rough-and-ready roll as it goes. The result is durable and quite tidy.

3. *Satin-stitch* is slow, but strong and very decorative. This is a particularly good method for lace which has not a pronounced pattern, or for doubled net hems, as in Fig. 65. In the latter case, slip the raw edge of the garment between the two thicknesses of net.

Slightly lap the plain edge of the lace over the raw edge of the stuff, both lace and stuff having right sides uppermost. Tack them together. With two or three strands of stranded embroidery cotton work a line of chain-stitch over the tackings. Cover this with close satin-stitch, taken into the lace on one side and into the stuff below it on the other. Finally, cut away any surplus stuff on the wrong side close to the stitches, being careful not to cut the stitches themselves.

4. *Lace-stitch* is not quick, but always looks lovely and delicate. To follow this stitch clearly, you should draw on a piece of paper an horizontal line, representing the join of lace and material. Place two dots a little above the line and two below it, in square formation. Label the upper left-hand dot *A*, the upper right-hand dot *B*, the lower left-hand one *C*, and the lower right-hand one *D*. Keep this diagram before you when practising the stitch.

Tack the lace to the right side of the stuff ½ in. below the raw edge. Begin by taking a backward stitch from *B* to *A*. Next, bring the needle through at *D*, and from there take a backward stitch to *C*. Bring the needle up again at *B*, and make a vertical stitch down to *D*. Then bring it out at *A*, and begin the process again with a backward stitch.

Now you begin to wonder if you have gone wrong, for you seem to be starting a second square with only three sides done of the first. Actually, while making the second square, you will automatically finish the first. When joining all the lace, cut away any surplus stuff close to the stitches on the wrong side.

Fig. 66 shows very much the effect of this stitch, forming a series of delicate little squares along the edge of the lace. In actual fact, this photograph is of *Roman-stitch*, which, though not quite

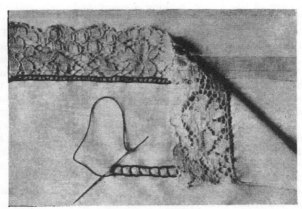

FIG. 66. *Above.* Lace attached by Roman-stitch and surplus
stuff being cut away on wrong side
Below. How to work Roman-stitch

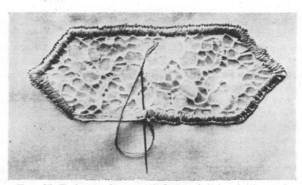

FIG. 67 To inset a lace motif, first tack it in position and
buttonhole its edges to the material

9—(H.2239)

44

as strong as lace-stitch, looks just the same on the right side, and is much quicker to work.

Tack on the lace as for lace-stitch. Or, if the material is fragile, crease a single narrow turn on the right side before tacking. Roman-stitch is a series of buttonhole stitches taken with a *slanting* needle. The method of working is shown at the bottom of Fig. 66.

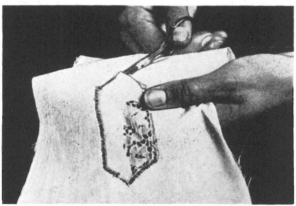

FIG. 68. Cutting away the material behind a lace motif after buttonholing it

The square effect is a result of taking each slanting stitch through the loop of the previous stitch, working rather loosely. Trim away the raw edge afterwards close to the stitches.

When turning corners with a lace edging, if this is gathered on, gather more fully round the corners, to prevent any dragging. If the lace is set on flat, mitre it neatly at each corner, pressing the tiny seams open. To mitre, fold and pin the lace at right-angles. Then make a diagonal seam from the corner of the lace to the corner of the garment. If necessary, sacrifice a little lace in order to match the pattern.

LACE-TRIMMED LINGERIE

To inset a lace motif right into the material, tack the motif into position on the stuff. With fine embroidery silk (preferably twisted) buttonhole the lace edges closely all round to the stuff (Fig. 67). Now with sharp embroidery scissors carefully cut away the material behind the lace right up to the stitching, leaving the lace transparent (Fig. 68).

For tucks, binding, rouleaux, shelling, and other trimmings used for underwear, refer to the chapters on frocks, or to the index.

UNDERWEAR EMBROIDERIES

THE embroidering of pale-coloured, silken undergarments is sheer fascination. You will enjoy it so much that I need hardly point out the additional inducements of this form of decoration—that it washes beautifully, usually wears longer than the garment, never gets out of order, and costs practically nothing.

With modern open stitches it takes very little time to do and requires very little skill. Neat fingers, a knowledge of elementary stitches, and an eye for colour will give lovely results.

No doubt you know the most ordinary embroidery stitches, such as satin-stitch, feather-stitch, French knots, and lazy-daisy. So, instead of taking up space describing them, I will pass to others, just as simple and pretty, which you are less likely to know.

Fig. 69 shows three for which you will find many uses.

Fly-stitch (top) is a form of buttonhole stitch. The photograph shows clearly how to work it, with the needle inserted diagonally, and the thread kept behind it, as in all buttonhole stitches. A little stitch over the point of the V is then made, as for lazy-daisy, to hold the V down. Fly stitch is very useful as a simple finish along hems and necklines. Two rows of it, the second reversed exactly over the first, gives a graceful diamond pattern.

Tuck-over stitch (middle row, Fig. 69) is a dainty combination of a tuck and an embroidery stitch, and can be used wherever a garment calls for pin-tucks. Tack a pin-tuck, either straight or in any desired curve, but instead of stitching it by hand or machine, overcast it with embroidery silk to the required depth, spacing your stitches out well.

Split-stitch (bottom, Fig. 69) is worked very much like the well-known stem-stitch. But it gains its name from the fact that, instead of the thread being kept below the needle, the needle

47

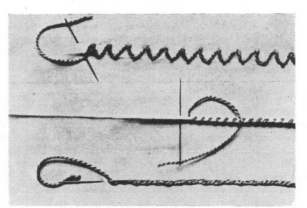

FIG. 69. *Top.* Fly-stitch. *Centre.* Tuck-over stitch
Bottom. Split-stitch

FIG. 70. A good example of the simple open embroidery
designs suitable for underwear

pierces it at each stitch. The result is a very "streamline" effect, like a closer and narrower chain-stitch. Use it where a thin line of colour is wanted, or for stems and fine outlines when embroidering designs.

Speaking of designs, Fig. 70 shows a good example of quick but effective lingerie embroidery, colourful, yet light and open.

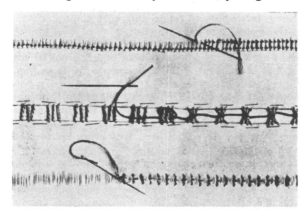

FIG. 71. Three open-work stitches. *Top.* Bar-hemstitching. *Centre.* Stack-stitch. *Bottom.* Single-crossing hemstitch

It is essential to keep embroidery on underwear really simple, for any elaboration is out of place on washing garments. Use outline and open stitches as much as possible, for they give the lightness of touch which is so appropriate to lingerie.

Drawn-thread and openwork hems and seams have just this airy effect, and, consequently, seldom go out of fashion for underwear. Every home dressmaker should be expert in working a few of the most effective openwork stitches, and three very pretty ones are illustrated in Fig. 71. Above and below are two forms of hemstitching; in the centre, a Parisian veining stitch, which will join curves as well as straight edges.

49

UNDERWEAR EMBROIDERIES

Bar-hemstitching (top). Draw threads to a width of ¼ in. or slightly less. Secure the embroidery thread. Put the needle behind the first four strands and pull the thread tightly round their base. Reinsert the needle at the starting side of the group of strands and make a little stitch into the solid stuff. Keeping the needle behind the first group, pass on and secure the next four strands in the same way, and so on all along. When one side is finished, turn the hem round and work the other side. Fig. 71 shows the second side being worked.

Stack-stitch (centre) gains its name from its likeness to piled stacks of corn. Press a narrow hem on each of the edges to be joined, and tack them on to stiff paper, as for faggoting, an even ¼ in. apart, ruling lines on the paper to guide you.

Take a straight bar stitch across the space from one edge to the other. Make two more bars, close to the first and each other, starting from each edge alternately. Leave a space equal to the width of the group of three bars, then work another group, and so on all along.

Start again with a matching or contrasting thread. Take it under the first trio of bars, over backwards, under again forwards, pulling the thread tight to give the stacked effect. Work similarly all along, carrying the thread on, unbroken, from one group to the next.

Single-crossing hemstitch (bottom) makes a very decorative border round pantie legs, square nightgown necks, or plain hems. Draw thread to the width desired, then secure the embroidery thread at the middle of one end. Pass the needle over six strands, then take up the next six, twisting the needle backwards under the whole twelve to form the crossed effect. Put the needle under the crossing, draw the thread taut, and continue.

The instructions in this chapter deal with the making and decoration of lingerie. Although daintiness should be the aim of the needlewoman in making up articles of lingerie, it should be borne in mind that most under-garments are subjected to quite a lot of strain, and all stitching of seams must be done very firmly. There are many ways of decorating articles of lingerie, and the methods include the insertion of fine net, inset or appliqué laces and ribbon, faggot stitching, drawn threadwork and various kinds of embroidery.

The seams for joining the parts of these garments may be hand sewn or machined. In most cases, French seams should be used to effect a strong and neat finish. Hems are usually stitched by hand, using fine silk thread or "Sylko," and working with a small hemming stitch, which only picks up one or two threads of the single material, but which picks a longer stitch on the turned edge, as illustrated in Fig. 17. Bias bindings are usually used in the same colour or with a contrasting shade to the garment. The bindings should be stitched by machine on the inside invisible edge, then turned over the edge and felled by hand. Bands of bias binding can also be faggot stitched to the garment if a more decorative effect is required, and to do this, a long strip of bias binding should be folded in half, lengthwise, and stitched together to make a long tube. The tube of bias binding should be turned right side out and pressed flat, and it should then be faggot stitched to the edge of the garment. There are many stitches which can be used for faggotting, and three popular examples of this form of work are illustrated in Fig. 17. It will be found best to tack the two edges to be joined, to a strip of brown paper, for ease in working. This helps to keep the distance between the stitches equal and prevents the material puckering. The examples of faggotting illustrated in Fig. 17 are described below.

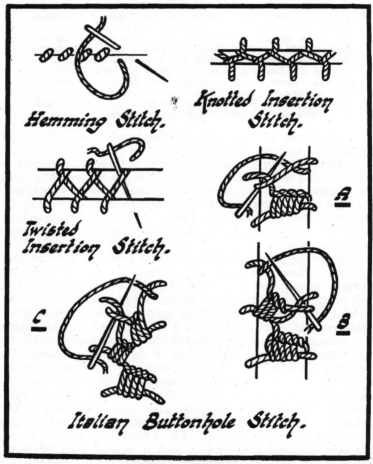

Fig. 17. STITCHES

Twisted Insertion Stitch: This very effective stitch should be worked from right to left. To commence it, thread a needle with strong thread or strong cotton, using only three or four strands of cotton. Join on at the edge at the right hand side of the band of bias binding, then leaving a space of one quarter to half an inch between, bring the needle through from the back of the main material and slightly to the left. To continue, take the needle under the thread, down to the band and take the stitch slightly to the left, to bring the needle through on the back of the band. Continue like this along the length of the work, always taking the needle under the thread of the stitch previously formed, before making a new stitch.

Knotted Insertion Stitch: This is a little stronger than the twisted insertion stitch, and it gives a firmer appearance. The knotted insertion stitch is worked from left to right along the band, and the same types of threads are suitable for use. To commence, join the thread to the band at the edge of the left end, then take a stitch slightly to the right in the main colour, bringing the needle through the top of the work to the underneath and taking the thread over the first thread, then take it under the point of the needle and pull it tight. Make a smaller stitch, slightly to the right of the lower band, and continue in the same way until the length of the band has been joined to the hem.

Italian Button-hole Insertion Stitch: This is a very difficult stitch to work, but if it is done properly and worked in a contrasting thread, it gives a very pleasing and lacy effect to the work, and is well worth the trouble. In working the stitch, the two edges of the pieces of material which are being joined should be tacked on paper, as previously described. The edges should be kept apart, at a distance of half an inch between them, and they should be parallel to each other. To work the stitch, the needle should be brought through at the top corner of the material on the right of the work, and taken across to make a bar to connect to the opposite corner of the other piece of material, as shown in the illustration, Fig. 17. Five button-hole stitches should be worked across this bar from left to right, as shown in the illustration, Fig. 17.

To continue, the needle should pick up the right edge of the material at a distance of about one quarter of an inch below the first stitch. It should then be brought across to the other opposite side, and another stitch made, slightly lower than the first stitch on this side of the work, to form a second bar. **Three** button-hole stitches should then be worked from the centre of the last bar outwards towards the right, and the needle should pick up the material on the lower side of the material, on the right side, about one quarter of an inch underneath. Three more button-hole stitches should be worked from the centre of this bar, outwards to the left side on the double thread. Then the needle should be worked, to pick up a piece of material on the same side, at a distance of about one quarter of an inch underneath the previous stitch. Continue from the centre outwards, to the right hand side, and work three button-hole stitches on the double thread and carry on in the same way, until the joining row has been completed.

French Seams: This method of joining the seams of articles of lingerie, is usually chosen, because it is easy to do. The seam formed is strong, and the finish is neat and eliminates the tedious work of neatening the edges of the seam after it has been worked. Also, French seaming provides a very neat finish on both sides of the work, and it is suitable for working on materials used in making lingerie. Although French seams are very suitable for making straight seams, they should not be used on curved seams because it makes them rather bulky.

To make a French seam, pin the two edges of the seams together, with the right side outside, and tack the pieces together very securely, not more than one quarter of an inch from the raw edges of the material. To continue, machine or hand stitch along the joining edges, using small running stitches and, with a pair of sharp scissors, neaten the raw edges and remove the tacking thread. Turn the garment on to the wrong side and press the seam so that it lies flat along the top of the fold, as shown in the illustration Fig. 17. Fell the raw edges between the two layers of material and tack these below them right along the seam, then machine or hand stitch with running stitch, just below the tacking, so that the raw edges are enclosed in the seam. It is sometimes necessary in a piece of work to define a cutting line or to draw attention to it, for instance, on a yoke and in this case, stitching should be made visible by forming a lapped seam.

Lapped Seams: In the illustration, Fig. 18, one piece of material is shown as being sewn over the other. When forming a lapped seam, it should first be decided which piece of the garment should lap over. To commence the seam, press a turning about half an inch deep on the wrong side of the overlapping piece of material, and place the folded edge half an inch over the raw edge of the joining piece of material with the right sides of both pieces uppermost. Pin first, then tack securely just above where the stitch line will be formed. Then, using a small neat back stitch, sew the parts together on the right side of the work. Turn the work to the wrong side, trim the raw edges to an even depth with a pair of sharp scissors, and overcast neatly.

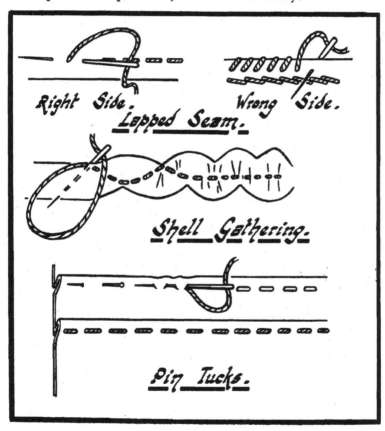

Fig. 18. LAPPED SEAM

There are many attractive and decorative ways of trimming lingerie, and a very simple and effective edging can be worked with shell gathering. Shell gathering, which is illustrated in Fig. 18, is made from the same material as the garment on which it is worked. It may be worked in the same colour, or a contrasting colour may be used for the shell gathering. Alternatively, ribbon may be used for the shell gathering, if a richer effect is required. Using silk material, a strip of material just over twice the length required and one inch wide, will be needed. If ribbon is used, a half inch width will be sufficient. The material should be gathered with both edges of the material on the wrong side, as illustrated in Fig. 18, and it should then be pressed well. To work the shell gathering, run a gathering thread along the folded material or ribbon, working diagonal rows of stitches alternately to the top and bottom edges of the strip, as shown in the illustration. This should be done to the ends of the strip, with the turning points at a distance of about one inch at both edges. When this is done, draw the gathering thread up, until it is in a straight line, and securely fasten the ends of the thread. Sew the trimming to the garment, through the centre line.

Pin Tucks: (See Fig. 18). These are used in lingerie for taking up the smallest possible amount of material. When they are worked in groups, the pin tucks give a very decorative finish, and they are also useful in this kind of work, for shaping the waist line of garments, when worked vertically. The finished effect depends on the evenness of the lines, and care must be taken in making up the tucks, to keep them of the same size. The material should be folded for each tuck exactly the same, and the pinning should be done as near the edge of the tuck as possible, with the work done on the right side of the material. When the tucks have been pinned, make a line of fine running stitches, not more than one-eighth of an inch from the fold. The pin tucks may be arranged in groups, and every tuck in the group should be exactly the same size, and parallel with each other.

Finishing treatments — scalloping — making patterns — working on thin materials — binding and facing — trimming and finishing — lace edging — cord edging — point turc — formation of the stitching — practise — working and finishing — making a nightdress — materials and method.

ONE of the most effective ways of finishing articles of lingerie is to work the edges in the form of scallops. Paper patterns may be obtained with scalloped edges, but if one has to make one's own patterns for scalloping, embroidery transfers which are produced with various size scallops can be obtained, or a cardboard pattern can be made, as shown in the illustration, Fig. 19. Pattern one edge of the cardboard shape, by cutting it into three or four curves of the required size. In use, the pattern should be placed on the material about half an inch from the edge to be worked, and the outlines of the scallops should be marked with a pencil.

When working scallops on thin materials, the best method of finishing is to bind the scallops with bias binding. If this is done, use as narrow a strip of binding as possible, and attach it as for ordinary binding. Stretch the binding a little when working in the corners and allow it to lie slack along the outer curves of the scallops, then turn the binding over and hem it down on the wrong side, as illustrated in Fig. 19. It may sometimes be found best to face scallops on thick materials. To do this, first tack the facing strip of binding along the edge to be scalloped, with the right sides of the materials facing. Mark the outlines of the scallops with pencil or chalk, but do not cut the material to the shapes of the curved edges. Pin both thicknesses of the material together, with a pin placed between each scallop, and the point towards the edge of the material, then make a line of backstitching along the pencil outline of the scallops.

To continue, cut away the materials from the scallops by trimming round the shapes with a pair of sharp scissors, leaving as narrow a turning edge as possible. With the scissors, snip between each scallop, nearly to the line of stitching. Turn the work inside out, and pin round the edges just below the edge,

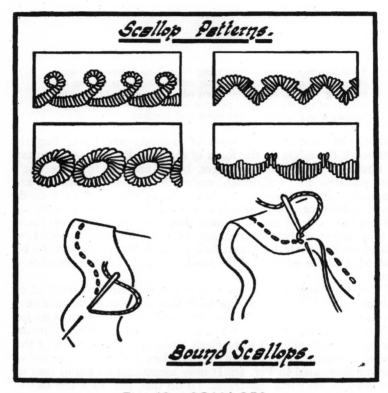

Fig. 19. SCALLOPS

working each scallop to a good shape, then tack along the edges and lightly press. After this, remove the tackings and press well again under a damp cloth. The raw edging of the facing should be fastened down with herringbone stitch, or it can be turned in and slip stitched.

The most effective trimming for lingerie is lace, and shaped lace motifs may be purchased, to form the yokes of nightdresses. These are best appliquéd to the garment, and finished by cutting the material away behind the lace motifs, so that the pattern of the lace is shown to its best advantage. Pin and tack the lace neatly into position, using small stitches. It is very important to ensure that the lace is held firmly in place during the stitching, or it may be moved or puckered. A line of running stitches worked round the edge of the lace with matching thread will assist in strengthening the finished article.

To continue, work narrow satin stitch over the running stitch on the outside edge of the lace, taking the needle right through the lace and the material to which it is to be attached. For this work, embroidery silk or stranded cotton matching the lace exactly, should be used. If stranded cotton is selected, use only two or three strands in the needle, and do not be tempted to match the thread to the fabric, as this will give the lace a heavy appearance.

A fine cord-like edging can be given to the lace, and to do this, lay an embroidery thread along the edge line of the lace, and work satin stitch over this thread. When all the lace has been appliquéd, turn the work to the wrong side and cut away the surplus material as close to the stitches as possible, taking care not to cut any of the threads of the lace.

Lace edging can be used to give a very dainty effect to underwear, although it is less decorative than appliquéd lace. A narrow lace edging, or wide lace with a straight edge, can be whipped to a garment to give a neat firm join with no raw edges. To do this, work with the wrong side of the material towards you, rolling the raw edge between the thumb and the first finger of the left hand, as illustrated in Fig. 20, then place the lace behind the material, with the straight edge of the lace at the top, and whip stitch the lace and material together, rolling the edge of the material as this is done. To continue, take the needle through the edge of the lace at the back, and through to the front just below the roll. When all the lace has been whipped to the material in this way, bring the lace up from behind the material at the seam, and fold down with a narrow ridge of whip, then press well. For the more ambitious needlewoman, point turc makes an unusual seam, which, in addition to being very strong, is also very decorative. Before attempting this seam on a garment, the stitch described below should be practised on odd pieces of material. There are five stages in the formation of this stitch, which is illustrated in Fig. 20.

To work the stitch, bring the needle through from the back of the material at point "A" as shown in the illustration, then insert the needle in the material again at point "B" in the illustration.

To continue, bring the point of the needle out again at "A", then draw it through and repeat this, so that there are two threads between points "A" and "B." To continue, take the needle to

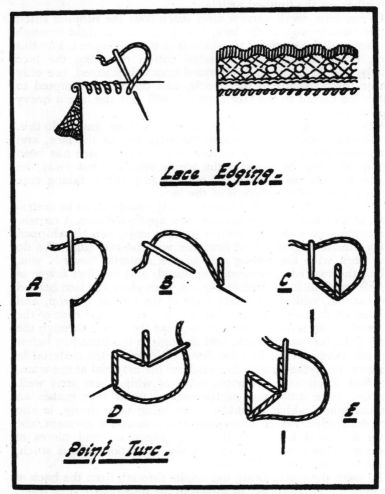

Fig. 20 LACE EDGING

point "C" which is in line halfway between points "A" and "B," and bring the needle out again at "A." Re-insert the needle at point "B" to make two threads between points "A" and "C" and bring it out again to the left at the point "D" as shown in the illustration. The distance between points "C" and "D" must be equal to the distance between points "A" and "B." After this, take the needle back to "C" and bring it out again at "D," making two threads from points "C" to "D." Re-insert the needle at point "A" and bring it out at point "D," as shown in the illustration. Draw the needle through and take it back to point "A," making two threads between points "D" and "A," but this time, bring the point of the needle farther along the stitch line to point "E," which will bring it into position to repeat the stitches.

Having practised the stitching on odd pieces of material, take the two pieces of the garment which are to be seamed together, and arrange and tack them as for commencing a lapped seam as previously described, then with a thick needle and thin sewing silk, work the stitch along the seam at the right side of the work. The thick needle will make a hole in the material where it enters and the silk should be pulled tight from hole to hole as the stitch is worked. Work the stitch over the folded edge of the seam and when it has been completed, trim away all the ends on the right side, as close to the stitching as possible.

To complete this chapter of working lingerie, a simple but graceful nightdress is described. This garment is illustrated in Fig. 21. The material required for the nightdress is three yards of thirty-six inch wide material. Select a soft material for the nightdress that will drape well. In addition to the main material you will require several yards of narrow ribbon. To make the nightdress, first cut the material into two equal pieces, then place the selvedges of both pieces together and join the two side seams.

Mark the centre of the front on the nightdress and turn over a hem about one inch deep all round the top edge, working two button-holes just below the hem and at the centre of the front as shown in the illustration Fig. 21, then turn the work to the wrong side and sew a casing of tape or bias binding along the hem and below it, and all the way round, beginning and finishing each side of the button-holes. Make plaits of the ribbon and stitch them into position for shoulder straps.

To continue, run a length of ribbon through the casing and

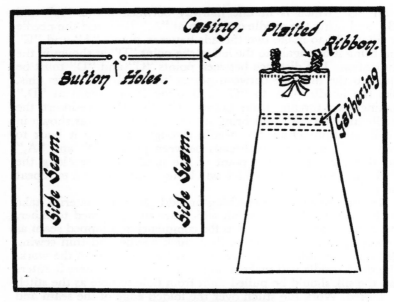

Fig. 21. NIGHTDRESS

bring the ends out through the button-holes on to the right side of the nightdress. It should then be tried on, and the ribbon should be pulled in to the correct measurement, and tied in a bow. The waist line should be marked next, and several rows of smocking or simple gathering should be formed across the front of the garment at waist level.

To complete the nightdress, sew ribbon ties on at each side of the smocking and turn up the hem of the nightdress, or if preferred, stitch a narrow lace edging round the bottom edge.

The pattern described is a very simple one, which can be made up with many variations of treatment.

LINGERIE

THOUGH the making of lingerie is not, technically speaking, dressmaking, the well-dressed woman will naturally see that her invisible garments are as dainty and shapely as her visible ones. However smart and becoming in themselves her frocks may be, their effect can be spoiled completely by being worn over badly-fitting lingerie. Paper patterns for underwear are modelled with as much care as those for upper garments, and should be selected quite as thoughtfully. Also, just as much care should be taken in their fitting and making, although the actual workmanship is simpler than in dressmaking, and a smaller equipment is needed.

MATERIALS

These should be light in weight and dainty in weave, though at the same time strong in texture and dye, in order to withstand the rigours of the laundry—unless, as so many women do, you wash your own lingerie; and even then some strain is unavoidable. So, when buying your materials, test them by pulling gently in both directions, and be sure that they are guaranteed fadeless, and also, in the case of woollens, unshrinkable. For " best " wear at its most luxurious there are georgette and ninon; when something less ephemeral is desired, silk, crêpe-de-chine, satin and rayon are available. (A good satin wears remarkably well, and is not really extravagant when its cost is balanced against its good qualities. Many a bridal gown of shimmering ivory satin has ended its career twenty years later as " nighties " and " knicks " !) For everyday wear lawns and cottons, either white or coloured, plain or patterned, are suitable, and may be most attractive. Broadly speaking, at the present time coloured fabrics are more favoured than white ones, though there are still many fastidious women who are faithful to fine white linen lawn trimmed with a little satin stitch embroidery or *broderie anglaise*, and perhaps a few real lace medallions. Others with similar tastes, though lighter purse, may use fine nainsook for everyday at least, with good crêpe-de-chine for slips and knickers. (Passée frocks of satin and crêpe-de-chine, either plain or patterned, can always be cut down into these garments.)

STITCHES

All stitching should be firm, in order to resist the strain of wear and washing; yet at the same time it should be as light as is consistent with strength, for clumsy stitching and coarse thread will prevent the effect of daintiness which is so desirable. Therefore strong but fine thread should be used in sewing, and both it and the size of the needles should be in keeping with the nature of the fabric. For all materials other than cottons fine sewing silk is unsurpassed, as it is more elastic than cotton, and therefore will not break so easily under strain. For white lawn or nainsook the thread may be no. 100, the needle no. 10 or 12, and the machine needle no. 11 or 12; for the same materials coloured mercerised matching cotton should be used, no. 40 or 50, with the same needles as before. For finer materials threads and needles should be proportionately finer, and, of course, sewing cotton or silk should always match in colour.

Some people consider hand sewing essential to the best class of work; but really, if the machining is done well and with a small stitch, there is no reason why the seams, at least, should not be done by machine, thus saving time and labour. Open seams, even with neatened turnings, are taboo; for, besides being untidy, they will not stand the strain of repeated washing. The seams most in use for thin fabrics are the French seam and the French fell, and in both of these the raw edges are enclosed. Run-and-fell seams are used only for the firmer materials, for which either of the previously mentioned seams would be too bulky.

FRENCH SEAM

How to make this is shown in Fig. 53, p. 103, and its making is described on p. 102. Each line of stitching should be pressed, and stretched slightly during the process (to counteract the tightening caused by the stitching) under a warm iron, before doing the next one. Remember in hand stitching to make every ninth or tenth stitch a back stitch for firmness.

FRENCH FELLED SEAM

This is even quicker to make than the previous seam, as it has only one row of stitching. It is illustrated in Fig. 54, p. 103, and described on the same page.

RUN-AND-FELL SEAM

Tack the two edges together on the fitting-lines on the wrong side, then stitch on the fitting-lines by machine from the side which will be on the top when the seam is finished, or from the under side if hand running is used. Cut off the under turning to $\frac{1}{8}$ inch, or more if the material is a fraying one; then turn down the upper turning over the lower one as narrowly as possible, folding in the raw edge, and tack close to the fold. Stitch by machine close to the fold, or fell by hand. (See Fig. 27, p. 58.) Note that in side and shoulder seams the front of the garment should be felled onto the back.

BEADED SEAM

This looks very charming for thin fabrics, using silk beading for silk, or " near " silk, and cotton for cotton or linen. Beading generally has a strip of plain material with raw edge at each side. Lay the beading right side downward on the right side of the material with the corded edge close up to the fitting-line, then run the two together close up to the corded edge. (See Fig. 140, p. 262.) Cut off the turning of the material a few threads beyond the sewing, and cut off the turning of the beading a little wider. Now roll the beading turning over the material edge towards you, and while doing so apply whipping stitch, working this over and over towards you and pushing off the little rolls from the eye of the needle so that this is never taken really out until the seam is finished. (See Fig 151, p. 285.) If the beading has no turning, tack it up

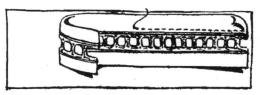

Fig. 140.—Applying Beading for Seam.

to the fitting-line as before described, then cut off the material turning and roll this over the beading edge with whipping stitch. Treat the other side of the seam in the same way, then press lightly with a warm iron. Lace beading, which has corded edges, may be applied similarly.

HEMSTITCHED SEAM
(by machine)

This can be done at any sewing-machine shop very cheaply, and is most satisfactory for very thin fabrics. Prepare the seams by laying one edge over the other and tacking through the fitting-lines, and the work will be returned to you with the hemstitching exactly over the tacking. (See Fig. 141A, p. 263.) Cut away the turning close up to the stitching on both sides, then press on the wrong side, stretching slightly at the same time. (Fig. 141B.) Be sure to tack with matching thread (silk or cotton, as the case may be), as the tacking-thread will be caught in with the machining, and cannot be removed. (It is usual to have any hems stitched to match, and how to prepare these will be described later.)

RULES FOR HEMS

The depth of hems varies with their positions. On the bottom of a petticoat-slip or nightdress,

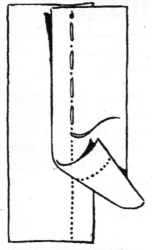

Fig. 141A.—Preparing
Hemstitched Seam.

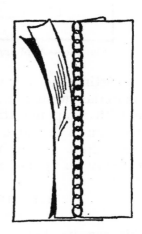

Fig. 141B.—Finishing
Hemstitched Seam.

for instance, from $\frac{1}{4}$ to 2 inches is correct, and other edges in proportion—according to fashion and the kind of material. As a rule the lower edge of these two garments is on the straight, or only very slightly curved, so that the tacking of the hem is an easy matter. In any case, the bottom of the hem should be turned first from the right side—one gets a better line that way—and tacked finely, close to the edge. Then on the wrong side the depth of the hem should be measured on the turning either with ruler, tape, or a notched card, and the turned-in edge tacked into place. If the edge is on a slight curve the resultant fullness on the upper edge should either be gathered finely or laid in small pleats to fit. The hem should be pressed lightly before being felled by hand with small stitches, taking up merely a thread of the outer material, with a double stitch at intervals on the turned-in edge for safety. If the hem is machined, it should be done from the right side as near the turned-in edge as possible, so that careful tacking is needed as a guide.

When a plain hem is used on transparent fabric, the turned-in part should be the full depth of the hem, so that it is three-fold.

A deep hem on a garment cut on the bias is not possible, and the lower edge may be finished with one not more than $\frac{1}{4}$ inch wide, or with one of the hems described later.

IMITATION HEMSTITCHED HEM
(by hand)

This may be worked on ninon or any soft, fine fabric without drawing threads. Tack a hem from $\frac{1}{8}$ to $\frac{1}{4}$ inch wide. Take rather thick thread and a coarse, blunt needle. Join on at the left end of the hem, then put the needle under the fold and bring out $\frac{1}{16}$ inch above. * Insert the needle in the single fabric close up to the fold and slightly to the right, so that the stitch produced is slanting; bring out the needle about $\frac{1}{12}$ inch to the left in the single fabric (making a perfectly straight stitch on the right side of the material), then pass the needle under the fold again and bring out $\frac{1}{12}$ inch from where the first stitch came out, and on the same level. Repeat from *. Pull the thread rather tightly

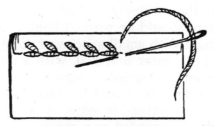

Fig. 142.—Imitation Hemstitched Hem.

so that rather large holes are made in the single material. (See Fig. 142.) Press on the wrong side.

HEMSTITCHED HEM
(by machine)

Tack the hem carefully, as for an ordinary plain hem, with the tacking as near the turned-in edge as possible, and using thread of the same colour as material, for the reason given in the instructions for a hemstitched seam. The finished stitch is the same as for the seam. When the fabric is transparent it is best not to turn in the raw edge of the hem, but to tack an even line $\frac{3}{8}$ inch below the raw edge. The hemstitching will come exactly over this tacking, and the raw turning must be cut away above it. Press on the wrong side and stretch slightly.

ROLLED HEM

This is only suitable for very thin materials, but it has a very decorative effect. The whipping stitch is shown in Fig. 30, p. 58, and the making of the hem is described on p. 108. It should be worked on the wrong side with rather coarser thread than is used for the rest of the sewing.

CROSS STITCHED HEM

This also is for thin fabrics, and a fairly thick thread should be employed. (It is illustrated in Fig. 143.) Tack the narrowest hem possible, join on the silk or other thread (which should be rather

Fig. 143.—Cross Stitched Hem.

coarse) at the right end, on the wrong side of the material. Then work over and over the hem with coarse but evenly-spaced stitches, bringing out the needle close up to the turned-in edge. When you get to the left end work back from left to right over the first set of stitches, crossing each perfectly. Do not pull the stitches tightly.

SCALLOPED HEM

This is only suitable for crêpe-de-chine and other thin materials. It is shown in Fig. 61, p. 109, and is described on the same page.

OTHER EDGE FINISHINGS

There are other edge finishings which cannot exactly be called hems, as they are more in the nature of trimmings.

BOUND EDGES

Either self material or one of contrasting colour or pattern may be used, but the strips must be exactly on the bias, and should be cut according to the directions given on pp. 68–9 (see Fig. 39, p. 69), and then sewn on in the way described on pp. 171–2. (If preferred, bias binding sold by the yard may be used.) When the material is very thin, the strips should be double—the double raw edges first being run onto the right side, and the fold being felled or slip hemmed to the garment on the wrong side just over the line of running, so that the stitches do not show on the right side.

Note that when the material is a stretchy one the joined-up strips should be stretched over the table edge before being sewn on, and especially if the edge being bound is on the inside of a curve, as on a round neck edge.

SCALLOPED EDGES

These are most attractive, and may be made in two ways : (a) bound with bias strips or (b) faced on the inside. For (a) see Fig. 106, p. 167, and the instructions on the same page; and for (b) see Fig. 107, p. 167, and the instructions on pp. 167–8. Note that when using (b) for lingerie the facing should be felled neatly instead of being slip hemmed, as the latter method is not firm enough to stand washing.

If liked, a fancy stitch such as chain stitch may be worked on the right side over the felled stitches.

BUTTONHOLED SCALLOPS

These are quite suitable for a thin material if it is firm and does not fray easily, otherwise the result does not repay the time spent on the work, and the scallops pull out of shape in washing. A very thin fabric, even though firm, may be faced on the wrong side with material cut to the shape of the edge and about 1 inch deeper than the scallops. The outer

Fig. 144.—Buttonholed Scalloping.

edges should be tacked level, leaving as much as possible outside the scallops to give a good " hold " for working, and the other edge of the facing should be turned in and felled neatly. A transfer may be used to mark the scallops, or their shape may be cut in brown paper round a coin—four or five in a row—and then the scallops may be drawn on the material round this pattern. When going round a curve, either outer or inner, some adjustment of the paper will be needed, either cutting or pleating it above or below the scallops so that their shape is not altered.

First run finely along the outlines of the scallops, then fill in the spaces between with running stitches. When working with silk, the padding may be done with matching cotton for economy. This running, besides rounding out the covering stitches, prevents the material splitting between the scallops. Now work over the padding with loop stitch (usually, though not correctly, known as buttonhole stitch), as shown in Fig. 144, p. 268, taking the stitches from left to right. Press the scallops on the wrong side over a padded surface, then with a sharp-pointed pair of scissors cut away the material outside the scallops from the back, being most careful not to cut the stitches.

FACED EDGES

When the edges are on the curve, hems are difficult, and facings are often substituted. If a different colour is used, they can be most decorative, as the second colour may be allowed to peep just $\frac{1}{12}$ inch or $\frac{1}{8}$ inch beyond the edge of the garment. Cut out the facing strips in the way described for bound edges, but when the edges are irregular it is best not to stretch the strips before applying them. Instead, when sewing the strip to an inner curve—for instance, a round neck curve—ease the strip very slightly, then turn the strip over and tack the edges level, stretching the other edge of the strip to allow it to fit the material below. If the edge of the facing is to project a little, then the strip must not be eased. When you are setting a facing on the outside of a curve, stretch the edge a little as you run it on, then, after turning the strip over onto the wrong side, you may need to ease it a little on the lower edge, or even to make tiny pleats here and there, to make the facing fit the diminishing width. But when the edge to be faced is very much curved or very irregular is is best to tack a piece of material to the right side of it, the two matching in grain, and with right sides together; then, after running round the outside edges, the facing should be turned to the inside of the garment and cut to an even depth before turning in and felling the raw edge.

APPLIED NET EDGES

First Method

For this it is necessary that the outside edges of the net should be straight, although the depth of the strip need not necessarily be equal all round. It is best to draw on paper the shape of the garment, and then mark on this the shape the net edge is to take. For instance, the garment edge may be applied to net in scallops in the following way. Stamp or draw the scallops on the material, and allow enough net to be fourfold and to go under the scallops with $\frac{1}{2}$ inch to spare. Fold the net once, then again, and make the fold meet the cut edges— it is now fourfold. Place the double fold to the outside edge marked on the paper and tack finely to the paper. Now lay the scalloped edge over the net, allowing as much net as you like beyond the scallops. Tack the material to the net and the paper, then run round the scalloped outlines through both material and net, using embroidery cotton or silk in accordance with the materials. Work the scallops as described for buttonholed scallops in Fig. 144.

Second Method

Here also the edge of the net should be on the straight thread, although the edge to which it is to be applied may be quite straight or very slightly curved. The finished width of the net should not be more than ¾ inch. Fold the net as before to make it fourfold, but when folding the second time let the raw edges project ⅛ inch beyond the fold, then turn them in and tack them level with the folded edge. Draw the shape of the garment edge on to brown paper, and from this measure the width of the net strip and draw a second line. Now tack the net to the paper, and when going round a curve stretch the net edge very slightly. Tack the other edge also. (This stretching should only be slight, as otherwise, when washed, the net will go to its original shape and the effect will be spoiled. If the curve is very marked, tiny pleats should be made and sewn to the neck.)

LINGERIE (*continued*)

EMBROIDERY

ALL the stitches needed for embroidering any material you may choose for your lingerie are described fully in *Teach Yourself Embroidery*, but it is well to remember that adaptation to the nature of the fabric is often necessary. For instance, when working on fine lawn, the embroidery thread must be fine and the stitches tight and well padded; while when using silk or crêpe-de-chine, a fairly coarse embroidery silk may be employed, and the designs may be freer in style, and not worked so finely. Though here, again, one must always consider future washings, and therefore not use stitches which may be disarranged easily either during this process or in the subsequent ironing.

FAGGOTING

Faggoting gives scope for originality in the trimming of lingerie—yokes, cuffs, neck edges, etc. It consists in joining together strips of material, ribbon, or lace insertion by means of fancy stitches, of which there is a great variety from which to choose.

First draw out on stiffish paper the shape you require the faggoting to be, but leave a few inches of spare paper all round. Now draw out the design on the paper. This may consist simply of bands following the shape of the outside edge of the paper, or it may be an arrangement of bands twisting and turning, leaving somewhat irregular spaces. But the width of the bands, varying from $\frac{1}{4}$ inch or less to $\frac{1}{2}$ inch, should be the same throughout the design.

In Fig. 145, below, you see a simple design for neck or sleeve edges; and, though the edge bands are shown on the straight, they may be adapted easily to a slight curve by stretching one edge of the

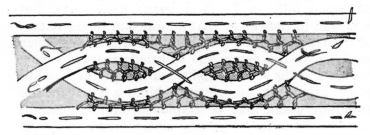

Fig. 145.—Simple Border in Faggoting.

strip as you tack it into place. The bands here consist of bias strips of crêpe-de-chine $\frac{3}{8}$ inch wide, although the width is just a matter of taste. Cut out the strips as previously described, making them twice the desired finished width plus $\frac{1}{4}$ inch for turnings. Join up the strips on their straight edges, press the turnings open, then fold the long strip with right side inside and raw edges meeting. Machine these raw edges together with $\frac{1}{8}$-inch turnings. Now attach a bodkin (or small safety-pin) to the seam at one end of the strip, leaving about 3 inches of double thread when joined on. Turn the bodkin back and insert it in the casing.

Push it along until you have turned out the strip completely and the bodkin emerges at the other end. (A similar method of turning a bias fold is illustrated on p. 172 in Figs. III A and B, though there a large safety-pin is used for a wider fold.) Now arrange the seam to come in the middle of what will be the under side, and press lightly with a warm iron on this side.

Tack the band to the paper in the position you have drawn out for it. One row of rather fine tacking-stitches is sufficient for a narrow band, but when wider than ⅜ inch, and when going round curves, both edges must be tacked. In this case the outer edge of the strip must be stretched slightly, and on the inner edge it may sometimes be necessary, though not always, to gather finely and draw up the thread to fit the curve. Sometimes it is better to make a tiny pleat instead of gathering, especially for a sharply-pointed corner. Now work across the spaces with the stitch D shown in Fig. 146, p. 276, though any one of the stitches shown in this Fig. may be used.

The thread used should be (for silk materials) twisted silk of the kind made specially for embroidering lingerie; for mercerised goods or plain cotton, tightly-twisted mercerised threads serve very well. A firm start should be made for the connecting stitch with a few tiny back stitches on the under side of the strip, and great care should be taken not to draw the stitches tightly, as even when they do not appear tight while the strips are on the paper they may do so when the strips are removed, so this fact should be borne in mind. As a rule the work is removed after all the strips have been joined, and is then neatened at the back and pressed; but at other times it is advisable to keep it tacked to the paper and attach the faggoting to the garment in that position. One's own discretion must be used as to which is the better plan in any particular case.

Faggoting Stitches

Four very useful connecting stitches are shown in Fig. 146, though it is an easy matter to find or invent others equally suitable.

A. Join on the thread at the right hand at the back of the lower strip. Bring out the needle at the front just below the folded edge. * Insert the needle in the upper strip, from the point exactly opposite where the thread came out on the lower strip; draw out the needle to leave a rather loose stitch, then pass it under the stitch thus made three times, and bring out in the lower strip close to where the thread came out, but slightly to the right. Draw up the thread, but not tightly, then insert the needle where it just came out and pass it along the inside of the fold from $\frac{1}{4}$ to $\frac{1}{2}$ inch to the left (according to the width of the strips), then repeat from *.

B. Join on the thread at the right hand in the lower strip, * take the thread straight across to the upper strip, and pass the needle to the back; bring out again in the same edge about $\frac{1}{8}$ inch to the left. Take a straight stitch across to the lower strip and

insert in the edge ⅛ inch from the first stitch. Pass
the needle along the back and bring out ⅛ inch to
the left. Repeat from *. Bear in mind that these
straight stitches must be decidedly loose and must

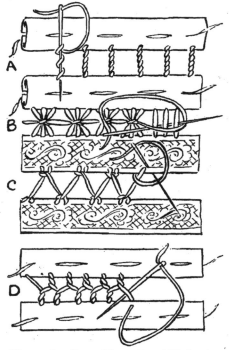

Fig. 146.—Some Faggoting Stitches.

be spaced perfectly evenly. When the whole
length has been done carry the needle to the middle
of the end stitch and fasten there, then turn the
work so that the stitches are horizontal. Hold
the thread coming from the fastening under the left

thumb just below the first three stitches. Insert the needle to the left of the thread above the top stitch and pass the point under the three stitches, bringing it out over the thread which is held under the thumb. Draw up the thread tightly to form a knot. Then repeat over groups of three stitches. Here again do not draw the thread tightly between the knots, or the finished effect will be ruined.

C. Work this with the strips running downward. Join on the thread at the top of the left strip, and bring out on the upper side about $\frac{1}{16}$ inch from the edge if a fabric strip is being used, or just inside the corded edge if insertion is employed. Hold the thread under the left thumb about $\frac{3}{4}$ inch below where it came out, insert the needle in the same edge about $\frac{1}{16}$ inch below where the thread came out, and bring out through the loop of thread. Carry the thread across slantingly to the other strip, and insert the needle about $\frac{3}{16}$ inch below the level of the stitch on the other side, and here make two little loops, as shown. Then carry the thread to the left strip at the same slant as before and repeat the two little loop stitches. Repeat as required. The beauty of this stitch lies in the regular slanting of the crossing threads.

D. Work this with the strips running across. Join thread to the left end of the upper strip, bringing out the needle on the upper side. * Carry the thread across to the lower strip about $\frac{1}{8}$ inch farther on to the right, pass the needle under it and bring out on the upper side. Pass the needle under the crossing thread from right to left, then insert under the upper edge about $\frac{1}{4}$ inch from where the first stitch was inserted, and bring out on the upper side. Pass the needle under the crossing thread from right to left as before, then repeat from *, keeping the stitches spread regularly.

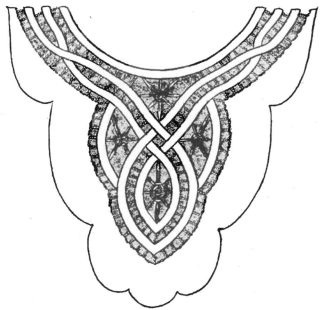

Fig. 147.—Dainty for Nightdress or Petticoat.

A More Elaborate Design (Fig. 147)

This makes a charming trimming for the front neck of a nightdress or petticoat-slip of crêpe-de-chine or satin. The strips are $\frac{3}{16}$ inch wide when finished, and are prepared in the usual way. The spaces are irregular in shape, and the connecting stitches must be adapted to suit them, being made longer and shorter, closer together or wider apart, as required. The joining stitch is that shown in Fig. 146 A, and when a large space occurs it is filled in with a spider web.

After the stitchery has all been done, the work should be pressed lightly on the back through the paper. The edge of the garment should next be cut to shape and prepared for attaching. It should be noted that allowance should be made for a space of from $\frac{3}{16}$ to $\frac{1}{4}$ inch between garment and trimming, and also that even when the garment appears to be set on plainly to the trimming, as in this case, yet really it should be allowed with a very slight fullness, or, when set on, it will appear skimpy. The garment edge should be hemmed very finely, or rolled and whipped. The edge should then be tacked to the paper, leaving the required space between it and the edge of the trimming.

In cases where a full edge is to be attached to the faggoting it should be rolled and whipped and drawn up to fit the faggoting with the required space left, and then tacked on carefully. After the connecting stitches have been worked (either the same as in the example or any other preferred), the faggoting should be removed from the paper and the under side made neat. All ends of thread should be fastened off, crossed bands should be made firm, and any raw edges turned in and felled neatly into place. Then the trimming should be pressed lightly on the wrong side.

Pinched Strips (Fig. 148)

These are very decorative, but bands must not be more than ⅜ inch in width before being " pinched ". After cutting and joining up the strips in the usual way, press them so that the join comes at one side. Join on the thread (usually the same as will be used for the faggoting) at the right end of the band; pass

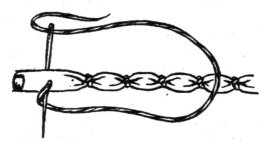

Fig. 148.—Making a Pinched Strip.

the needle and thread along the inside of the band and * bring out in the middle of it on the upper side, about ½ inch to the left. Then put the needle behind the band from the top and bring it out below the edge; hold the thread coming from the hole under the left thumb and carry it under the point of the needle from left to right. Now with the right hand draw up the thread tightly through the loop. Put back the needle through the knot thus made, pass it along the inside of the band, and repeat from *. Note that the knots should be drawn tightly, but the thread between them should be left easy.

APPLIQUÉ

Appliqué makes charming trimmings, which are at the same time durable, on crêpe-de-chine and other materials of fine, even weave, especially when two pale shades are used together—for instance, pink on blue, or mauve on pink, etc. The designs should be simple and have smooth, not serrated,

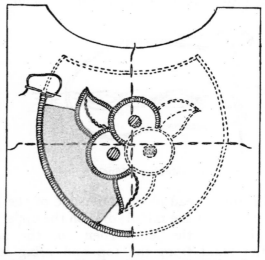

Fig. 149.—Appliqué Trimming for Lingerie.

edges, as the former are better for washing and wear. The usual methods of appliqué are described in *Teach Yourself Embroidery*, but it is well to remember that for lingerie the stitches should be small, even, and set closely together—preferably buttonhole stitch or padded satin stitch. But there is another method which may be described here, which, while not strictly appliqué, produces a similar effect.

In Fig. 149, p. 281, you see a trimming which could be used for front neck of petticoat-slip or night-dress or for nightdress sleeves or the sides of knickers. A motif of the same material as the garment rests upon a background of similar material, but in another colour, or of white or cream net, and is enclosed in a line of buttonhole stitch to form a circle, shield, or other suitable shape. You can easily draw such a design yourself, using a penny as a guide for the three circular flowers, and drawing the leaves freehand; or, if you prefer it, it is easy to buy a similar transfer. If you use one of these, iron it off on to the garment in the desired position; but if you draw your own design, outline it with a fine pencil on tracing paper, then lay a piece of carbon paper in the correct position for the design and place the tracing paper over the carbon. Trace the outlines with a hard, firm pencil, and be most careful that your fingers do not press over the carbon, or irremovable marks will be made. (In the case of new carbon papers, some of the colouring matter should first be removed with a soft rag or tissue paper.)

If you are using the same material, but of a different colour, for the background, cut a piece large enough to cover the outside edges of the space and with a spare 2 inches all round it. Be sure to match the garment material in weave. If you are using net, cut it in the same way, but double. Whichever you use, place it *under* the design on the garment, allowing an equal margin all round the outside line. Tack to the garment first from top to bottom, then from side to side, then tack again at each side of the first line at a distance of 1 inch; then again twice across, equally spaced. Finally run together round the outside line rather finely.

Now work round the outlines of all parts of the motif in tight buttonhole stitch over one or two lines of fine running in the embroidery thread, keeping the corded edge to the outside. Be careful to take all stitches right through both layers of material. Use fine corded silk for silk materials or twisted cotton for cotton goods. (This should match the material of the garment in colour.) When all this has been done work round the enclosing line in the same way, but with the corded edge of the stitch on the inside. Work the ribs of the leaves in outline stitch, and the roundels in the middle of the flowers in padded satin stitch. Then take a pair of fine-pointed scissors and cut away the material (upper only) between the motif and the enclosing buttonholing, as in Fig. 149. Press lightly on the wrong side.

LACE TRIMMINGS

These may be in the form of medallions, motifs, edging, insertion, etc. In any case, choose strong lace which will last as long as the garment, otherwise much labour is expended in renewing the trimmings while the garment itself is still in good condition. How to apply medallions, edging, and insertion is described on pp. 173-4 under the heading Lace. You will find an illustration of the second method of applying insertion in Fig. 150 A and B. Here note that at the crossing of the insertion the under piece is cut away and the raw edges are turned back and run to the upper piece, but when the lace is very fine this is not necessary.

There are also very attractive machine-made laces of artificial silk on net in white, ecru, and

Fig. 150A and B.—Applying Insertion.

A   B

Right Side.   *Wrong Side.*

colours. They include yokes, motifs, neck and sleeve trimmings, etc., and are suitable for use on any of the silk (real or artificial) fabrics sold for lingerie. To attach them, lay the garment, right side upward, on a flat surface and place the lace over it, also right side upward. Pin together in many places, then tack carefully, and be sure not to get either lace or garment tight upon the other. Take silk matching the lace in colour, and work tiny stitches from the material over the edge of the lace. These stitches should be very close together and as small as possible. After this has been done turn to the back and cut off the turnings to $\frac{1}{8}$ inch or less. Oversew the raw edges, or loop stitch them, to prevent fraying, or, if preferred, turn them under and fell very finely to the lace.

EMBROIDERY EDGINGS AND INSERTIONS

When the edging is narrow and is to be set onto the garment plainly—for instance, on the edge of the round neck of a nightgown—it is usual to place a beading between the edging and the garment.

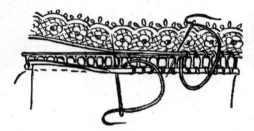

Fig. 151.—Applying Beading and Edging.

The beading can be set on as described in Chapter **XX** for a beaded seam (see Fig. 140, p. 262, and Fig. 151 on this page). When there is no material left on the beading, place the beading right side downward on the right side of the material, with the latter projecting about $\frac{1}{8}$ inch above the corded edge. Then roll this little turning toward you over the corded edge and whip the two together the reverse way—that is, with the beading facing you and the material turning rolled over the corded edge.

To apply the embroidery edging to the beading, cut off the required amount of plain material, then proceed as just described. In Fig. 151 the edging

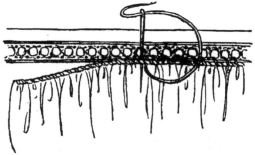

Fig. 152.—Whipping Fullness to Beading or Insertion.

is lace, so the work is even simpler, and the needle is inserted from the back instead of from the front.

When setting on beading to full material, the latter should be rolled and whipped as described on p. 58, then the two must be whipped together as in Fig. 152.

Applying Embroidery Insertion

There are at least three ways of applying embroidery insertion.

A. If the insertion is to have plain material at

Fig. 153.—Applying Embroidery Insertion to Plain Edge.

each side, place the embroidery with right side to right side of the material, and run together finely. Then cut off the turning of the garment to $\frac{1}{16}$ inch, and that of the insertion to a thread or two more. Roll over the two edges towards you, and then use the needle as in Fig. 153. The other edge of the insertion may be applied to plain material in the same way, or may be whipped to beading or edging as before described for beading.

B. When the insertion has a corded edge, cut off the plain material close up to it, then tack the insertion with its right side to that of the material; but leave a little turning of the latter above the insertion. Roll this turning toward you over the insertion and whip together in the usual way.

C. Enclose the insertion in a French seam. Place the wrong sides of insertion and material together and run or machine them just under $\frac{1}{4}$ inch from the insertion edge. Cut off turnings as far as is safe, turn to wrong side, and run or machine close up to the insertion edge.

PICOTING

First read the paragraph on this subject on p. 175. It is possible to have almost the whole of a garment made at the machine shop—seams and hems being hemstitched, and any frills and neck and sleeve edges finished with picoting. This is quite satisfactory when very thin fabric such as ninon is in use. The seams must first be tacked, but not as for hand-sewing. One edge should be laid flat over the other as shown in Fig. 141A, and a line of tacking made through the two fitting-lines. If the lower edge is to be picoted, the line for this must be tacked, leaving at least 2 inches below. But if there is to be a hemstitched edge, this cannot be done until the seams have been treated, and so a second visit to the machine shop will be necessary. Any edges, such as those of frills, must be tacked along the fitting-line; turnings of from $1\frac{1}{2}$ to 2 inches should be left, and where any edges are much curved they should be tacked onto tissue paper. But if a good length of frilling is needed and a large piece of material is available, a simpler way is to measure the frilling on this with a ruler, so as to get the exact depth, and to tack the dividing lines finely. The stitch will be worked on these lines, and all that will be needed is to cut through the stitching.

When the garment returns, cut off the seam turnings on both sides as close to the stitching as possible, but on any outside edges cut through the middle of the stitching. Hems may be tacked with either a single or a double turn. If the former, then tack up at an even height all round above the lower edge of the garment, leaving a turning of at least 1 inch above the tacked line; if the latter, make the two turns of the same depth when the fabric is transparent, then tack close to the turned-in edge; but when the fabric is not transparent, the raw edge should be turned in for at least $\frac{1}{4}$ inch. The hemstitching will then come half on the hem and half on the single material. One thing should always be remembered—that is, always to tack for hemstitching or picoting with matching thread, as it will be caught in with the machining and cannot be removed.

TUCKS

Full directions for making several varieties of tucks are given on pp. 153–6, and any one of these is suitable for lingerie, with the exception of corded tucks. Tucks are often alternated with lace or embroidery insertion with good effect.

PLEATS

These are not used much for lingerie, except for the fullness which is often placed in the side seams of petticoat-slips to give ease for walking and yet at the same time preserve a slim outline. Inverted pleats are most suitable here, and they are described on pp. 161–2.

GATHERS

Read the instructions for gathers on p. 166. Note that most of the materials now in vogue for lingerie are sufficiently supple to allow the stroking stitch to be dispensed with, though this is necessary with the old-fashioned stout fabrics such as long-cloth or cambric. This stroking, when it must be used, is worked in the following way.

Mark off the edge to be gathered in quarters to correspond with similar marks on the band or edge to which the gathers are to be joined. Then gather on the fitting-line (see Fig. 25, p. 56). A second row of gathers *above* the first makes them set better. Draw up the threads fairly tightly and twist them

K (Dress)

round a pin which is set in point downward at the left end. Hold the gathers in the left hand, and with the eye of a coarse sewing-needle or the blunt end of a wool needle press each little fold into place against the thumb of the left hand, working from left to right. This stroking must be done very gently, and on no account should the sharp point of a needle be used, or the material will be scratched and its surface ruined. Stroke in the same way on the wrong side, then let out the gathers to the required width.

Setting Gathers Into a Band

When setting gathers of stout material into a waist-band or sleeve-cuff, etc., proceed as follows :

The waist- or sleeve-band will be cut out with the warp threads running round the figure for strength. If the band is to be in the form of a ring, join up the ends on the wrong side and press the turnings open; if the ends are to be open, fold the band down the middle on the wrong side and join up each end. Now in either case turn up $\frac{1}{4}$ inch or less on each edge of the band. Quarter the band and mark with pins, then match up with the quarterings on the gathered edge, and pin together there. Lay the turned-up edge of the band over the gathers on the right side so that the lower gathering thread is just covered. First pin into place, then tack finely through the folded edge. Now fell the folded edge between the gathers—one stitch to each gather—producing upright stitches. When finished, turn to the wrong side and tack in the same way, except that the fold should come the slightest bit higher than on the right side in order that the second set of felling stitches will not show through on the right side.

When Using the Sewing Machine

After letting out the gathers to the desired width, take the band and crease one edge only; then lay this right side downward on to the right side of the gathers and tack very finely through band and gathers on the creased line, which should come exactly over the lower gathering thread. Now turn the garment to the wrong side and turn up the band on the lower edge; then tack it over the gathers with the fold just a shade below the fold on the right side. Now stitch from the right side close to the fold of the band; and if the ends are open, then carry the stitching up the ends also.

For Very Thin Fabrics

For the thin fabrics, now generally used, the gathers are usually set into bands similarly to the method used for machining just described, but with a fine running stitch over the first row of tacking (before the band is turned up), and felling on the wrong side, as for the hand-sewn method. But when the fullness is set onto a single edge it must be done by rolling and whipping.

Waist Fullness at Side of Petticoat

In a princess petticoat or slip there is often a horizontal cut on the waist-line at each side of the under-arm seam, into which fullness on the lower edge is set. Stitch the side (under-arm) seams as you prefer—usually French seams—then take two bias strips of the same material ¾ inch wide. Place one strip on the upper side of the cut with right sides together and raw edges level; tack the two together. Turn to the wrong side and tack the other strip over the cut in the same way, then run or machine together as close to the raw edges as is

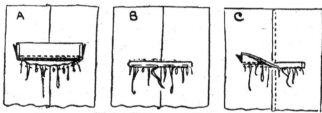

Fig. 154.—Waist Fullness at Side of Petticoat.

safe (see Fig. 154A). Gather the lower edge to fit the upper, then turn in the edge of the strip on the right side and tack it over the gathers. Fell this into place by hand, or machine close to the turned-up edge (see Fig. 154B). Tack down the strip on the wrong side in the same way and fell into place (see Fig. 154C).

SMOCKING

This may often be employed in lingerie, particularly when the gathering is fine and the fancy stitches firm and close, so that they do not get disarranged in washing. (Smocking, of course, is always in favour for children's frocks, and from time to time it is fashionable for blouses for adult wear.)

The amount of fullness required for smocking

varies with the thickness and texture of the material, and also with the stitches to be used. The average amount required is three times the width of the finished measurement, but thicker materials will not need so much fullness, and very fine ones can take more.

Preparation

The preparation of the material for the fancy stitching, by means of rows of gathers, is all-important. To ensure perfect regularity there are two methods.

1st Method. Buy a transfer of rows of evenly-spaced dots. On fine materials the dots should be from $\frac{1}{4}$ inch to $\frac{3}{8}$ inch apart, while on thicker ones $\frac{1}{2}$ inch is usual. See to it that the top edge of the material is cut by a thread. Place the transfer on the *wrong* side of the material with the rows of dots on the straight thread.

Calculate how many rows of gathers you will need for the fancy stitches and add one extra for the top row, which will usually be set into a band of some kind. Tack the paper into place on the *wrong* side of the material with the row of dots on the same thread, then apply a hot iron.

2nd Method. Take a ruler and pencil or chalk and rule horizontal lines the required distance apart, keeping on the straight thread. Now cross these lines with downward ones to form perfect squares.

The Gathering (Fig. 155)

This is done on the wrong side with fairly thick but soft cotton. Make a large knot on the cotton,

which cannot be pulled through the fabric. Now
begin at the right hand by taking a stitch under a

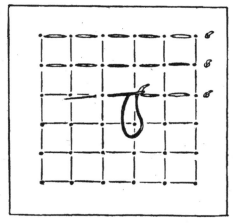

Fig. 155.—Foundation Gathering for Smocking.

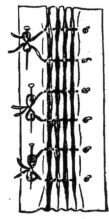

Fig. 156.—Draw-
ing up the Gathers.

few threads exactly on the dot or
at the crossing of the lines on the
squares. Continue to the end of
the row, and here cut the cotton,
leaving about 1 inch. Repeat until
all the rows have been gathered,
then make an extra row about
$\frac{1}{8}$ inch above the top row, taking
up the threads immediately above
the stitches of the row below.
(This extra row gives firmness.)
Now draw up two threads at once
from the left hand and twist them
together round a pin placed verti-

cally at the end of the two rows. Repeat until all the rows are drawn up to an equal width (Fig. 156). This should be almost as much as the desired finished width.

Planning the Stitches

It is necessary to have a clear plan in your mind before beginning the fancy stitches. This can then be drawn out on squared paper and consulted as you work. Almost any fancy embroidery stitch can be used—most usually outline, crewel, feather, chain, etc.—and some of the elaborate patterns are simply arrangements of one or two stitches in diamonds or waved lines. They are not difficult to carry out, but they entail careful counting of stitches and folds on the material so that a whole pattern, or else the division between two patterns, comes in the exact middle of the finished work.

Holding the Work

The material may be held in the left hand while being worked, or it may be tacked carefully to a piece of stout but pliable paper, and then the gathers should be stretched out to the exact width desired. Some stitches are worked from right to left, some from left to right, and for some others—such as chain stitch—the work must be turned so that the little folds come horizontally and the stitch is worked downward.

Fig. 157

This is a simple pattern to start with, being merely an arrangement of crewel, outline, and chain stitches.   Ten rows of gathers are required, with an extra row worked ⅛ inch above the top row for strength.   These two will not be worked on.   Work a row of crewel stitch on the second and fourth gathered rows, and a row of chain stitch on the third

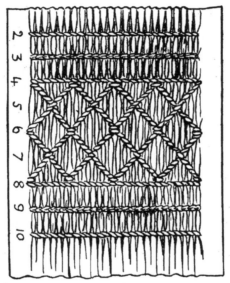

Fig. 157.—A Simple Pattern for a Start.

row of gathers.   Repeat these on the eighth, ninth, and tenth rows of gathers.   In the space left work a trellis band as follows :

Begin close up to the straight row of crewel stitch at the left hand.   Bring out the needle to the left of a fold and * work outline stitches in a slanting row, making the fifth stitch exactly on the fifth gathered row, and bringing out the needle after the ninth stitch exactly on the sixth gathered row. Now work nine crewel stitches slanting upward to the straight crewel row. Repeat from *. Next start with a stitch on the sixth gathered row exactly underneath the first stitch of the previous slanting row of stitches. Now work a slanting row of crewel stitches to the fourth gathered row, immediately in the middle of the space. Then continue working downward and upward to cross the previous rows of stitches to form diamonds and triangles. Now repeat what has just been worked on the sixth, seventh, and eighth gathered rows.

Here is a reminder that when working outline stitch horizontally from left to right the needle is brought out *below* the previous stitch, while when working the same vertically the needle is brought out to the *right* of the previous stitch. But when working crewel stitch horizontally the needle is brought out *above* the previous stitch, while when working vertically it is brought out to the *left* of the previous stitch.

The border is finished with three rows to match the upper part of the border—a row of crewel stitch on the eighth and tenth gathered rows, and a row of chain stitch on the ninth gathered row.

Fig. 158

Eight gathered rows are needed for this pattern, adding an extra row for firmness immediately above the top row—neither of these being worked over, and not being shown in the diagram. Work over the second and fourth gathered rows in crewel

stitch, or outline, if preferred, and work over the
third gathered row in single feather stitch.* Join
the thread at the left hand close to the last row
of crewel stitch, and bring out the needle to the left
of a fold. Work five slanting outline stitches down
to the next (the fifth) gathered row; then work
upward to the fourth gathered row with five crewel

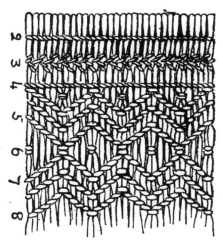

Fig. 158.—Waved Lines are Effective.

stitches. Repeat from * as required. (See that
the triangles thus formed are equally spaced.) Now
join on to the beginning of the fifth gathered row
and work as before between this and the sixth row,
and when this is done work another row midway
between the last two rows. After this join the
thread on the seventh gathered row immediately
under the first stitch on the fifth gathered row and
work three waved rows as before, but in reverse, so

as to form a row of diamonds between the two sets of three. Exactly in the middle of each diamond catch the two middle pleats together with two back stitches; finish off each pair of stitches separately so that the thread is not carried across at the back.

Honeycombing

This is the most elastic stitch of any used in smocking, and it may be used entirely by itself or combined with others. Fig. 159 shows exactly how it is worked. Bring out the needle to the left of a fold at the left hand of the work on the second gathered row. Take two back stitches over this fold and over the one to the right of it, and when making the second stitch insert the needle downward through the fold to the next gathered row, bringing it out there to the left of the second fold (which will be the first of the second pair). Now catch together this fold and the one to the right, as in the previous stitch, but in the

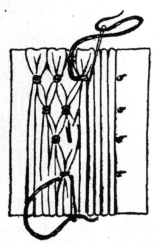

Fig. 159.—How to Work the Honeycombing.

last stitch pass the needle upward to the previous gathered row and bring it out to the left of the fold. (Both these movements are shown in Fig. 159.) Repeat these stitches on the two gathered rows alternately. To work subsequent rows repeat on the gathered rows below, either in the whole width of the material or in sets of diminishing stitches to form a vandyke pattern as in Fig. 160.

Fig. 160

Fourteen gathered rows are required for this, with an extra one just above the first—these two are not worked on, and are not shown in the diagram.

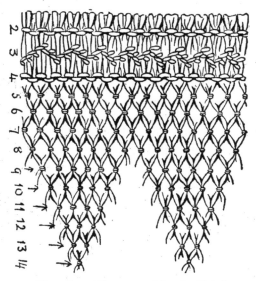

Fig. 160.—Honeycombing in Points.

Work cable stitch over the second and fourth rows. This is similar to crewel stitch, but the needle is brought out above and below the previous stitch alternately. Work double feather stitch over the third gathered row. Honeycombing is worked over the next four gathered rows right across, and then the points are formed over the remaining six gathered rows.

Embroidery Threads

For lingerie it is well to choose a rather tightly twisted silk or cotton, with its thickness in proportion to the texture of the material. Stranded cotton may frequently be used, with the number of strands appropriate to the pattern and fabric. A fine crewel needle is the best to work with.

Finishing Off

After all the fancy stitches have been worked, and before taking out the gathering threads, place the work on an ironing blanket with wrong side upward. Pin out the edges straight, then place a damp cloth over the back of the work and pass the iron lightly over it. On no account press the work, or the whole effect will be spoiled. Then remove the damp cloth and hold the iron over the material, but not touching, until the steam has evaporated. Leave for a few minutes, and then withdraw the gathering threads. This process sets the gathers and gives a professional look to the work.

LINGERIE (*continued*)

FASTENINGS

BUTTONS and buttonholes or buttons and loops are the most usual fastenings for lingerie. Hooks and eyes are taboo, and although press studs are sometimes seen on crêpe-de-chine and satin slips and petticoats, these neat little fastenings are frowned upon by experts on account of their unsuitability for washing.

Buttons and Buttonholes

Buttons for lingerie are generally either small pearl ones or small unpierced linen ones—the latter for lawn and cotton fabrics. The pierced linen ones are never used on dainty garments, and in any case buttons should always be as small as efficiency permits, for large ones are both clumsy and out of place, and are calculated to mar the beauty of an otherwise attractive and well-made garment. The buttons should be sewn into position before the holes are cut, or their positions should be marked with pencil or cross stitches, and the spaces between should be measured carefully with a ruler. (When many buttonholes are to be made, it is a good thing to space the positions out on cardboard and thus make a gauge to cut them by.) Buttons and buttonholes should, with very rare exceptions, always be on double material, and when there are several in line, as for instance on front, back, or side fastenings, the edges should either be hemmed back or faced with a strip of self-material. When the buttons and buttonholes are isolated, so that neither hem nor facing is practicable, a small square of material cut on the same grain as the button or buttonhole site should be placed beneath it and felled all round.

Use strong double silk or cotton, according to the material, for sewing on buttons. First make two small back stitches on the button site on the right side of the material, then place the button exactly over them and bring up the needle and thread through one of the holes in the button. Place a pin across the button and take the stitches over it. When there are four holes, make a cross of two stitches each way; if there are two holes, make four stitches across, then pass the needle to the back of the button, between it and the material; withdraw the pin and twist the thread three or four times round the sewing-on stitches to form a "neck". Pass the needle to the back, make one or two back stitches and cut the thread (see Fig. 71, p. 123).

For Shank or Covered Buttons

Moulds are sometimes covered with a circle of the garment material—this being gathered round the edge and drawn up into the centre of the under side. For these, and for buttons with a shank, the method of sewing is to start as before with small back stitches, then to pass the needle through the shank (or through the gathered covering of a mould), and then through the material and back again, repeating this as required for strength. In the case of a covered button a " neck " should be made as described for the button with holes.

For Linen Buttons

When linen (unpierced) buttons are used, begin work on the button site with two back stitches, then place a pin across the button and bring the needle out on the top. Carry the single thread four times over the pin and across a little space not more than one-third the width of the button and exactly in the middle of it; then bring the thread to the right side, remove the pin, and work loop stitch over the strands (as shown in Fig. 76, p. 129); make a " neck " as before, and secure the end of the thread.

Buttonholes

These are like those used in dressmaking, but not in tailoring. When the buttons have been sewn on, place the buttonhole side of the opening over them and mark the place of each button with a pin. Now either chalk or pencil the line for each buttonhole, using a ruler. The buttonholes should be on the straight thread, if possible, though this cannot always be managed, and if not, care must be taken that the slits are not stretched, and to prevent this it is wise to overcast the slit very lightly. The length of the slit should be $\frac{1}{16}$ inch more than the width of the button, if this is a flat one; if it is a dome-shaped one, then $\frac{1}{8}$ inch more. (But it is a good plan to cut experimental slits in a spare piece of material to make sure.) The distance of the buttonholes from the edge of the material should be enough to allow ⅛ inch, at least, beyond the buttons when they are fastened, so that this all depends on their size. Cut each slit as required, to avoid stretching.

Method of Working

Coarser thread than is used for the sewing of the garment should be employed for the buttonholes, and silk on all materials except cotton ones. (See Fig. 73, p. 127, for method.) Stitches should be as short as is compatible with strength, and they should be placed closely together with not more than a hair's breadth between them. The thread should be drawn up tightly to make a good knot after each stitch, and so that this knot comes exactly on the edge of the slit; but it should not be drawn up *over-tightly,* or it will tear the fabric.

To begin, secure the thread at the left end (that farthest from the edge of the material). Bring out the thread there just below the cut and begin to work the stitches from left to right as shown. After inserting the needle, take the thread coming from its eye and draw it round under the point from the left side, then draw up the needle to form the knot. When you reach the other end fan out the stitches (five or seven), and continue along the other side until you reach the starting point. Here pass the needle into the slit and out again at the beginning of the first stitch you made. From there take two or three stitches across the end of the buttonhole and bring out the needle at the left hand again. Then work buttonhole stitch over these strands, keeping them free of the material. Pass the needle to the back and finish off there. When making button-holes downward (as for the front fastening of a shirt blouse) both ends must be barred.

Buttons and Loops

When the material is not firm enough to serve as a foundation for buttonholes, loops should be used instead. The buttons should be sewn on as before, and the position of the loops marked accordingly on the other side of the opening. Sometimes (*a*) the loops are made just under the edges so that the buttons are covered, and at others (*b*) they are made on the extreme edge. You must make your own choice. In any case the right side should be hemmed or faced to make it double.

Method A

Attach the thread for the loop to the left end of the right side of the garment (holding the edge to-wards you). Bring out the thread for the loop just under the edge and carry a strand across the space for the loop, which should be the width of the button. Leave this strand very slightly loose from the material. Make a tiny stitch through the fabric, then ,carry the thread back again to the starting point and take a tiny stitch there. Now test the loop over the button and adjust if necessary. Carry two more strands across in this way, and then work over them in loop stitch (see Fig. 76, p. 129). When you finish at the right-hand end you may fasten off there with a few tiny back stitches, or, if you have enough thread, you may pass the needle through the material and bring it out at the next position and repeat.

Method B

Work as before, but on the extreme edge. Note that when round or dome-shaped buttons are used a looser loop will be needed, but this can only be decided by experiment.

Cord Loops

These are made in the same way as for dress-making (described on p. 128 and illustrated in Fig. 75), but with one slight difference—in lingerie the edge for the cord must be hemmed before the cord is sewn on.

CASINGS FOR ELASTIC

These are needed at the waist and knees of directoire knickers. When the edge is on the straight, tack a hem one-and-a-half times the depth of the elastic, and stitch by machine on both top and bottom of the hem—hand sewing is not firm enough. Make an opening for elastic, preferably by unpicking the little bit of seam in the hem at the centre-back of a waist edge, or at the inside seam of knee edge. Buttonhole the edges of the opening. When there is not sufficient material for a hem, or the edge is curved, cut a bias strip twice the width of the elastic. Turn down and press the edge of the garment, then do the same to the raw edge of the bias strip and tack it just below the turned-down edge of the garment. Arrange the opening to come at the ends of the strip at the place suggested for a hem. Turn back both ends of the strip and button-hole them as before. Turn up the other edge of the strip and tack it into place, then stitch on both edges as near the turn as possible.

Inserting Elastic

Pin a small safety-pin to one end of the elastic and run it through the casing. Join the ends of elastic by overlapping them for $\frac{1}{2}$ inch and sewing firmly all round. If there is a small placket in the garment the elastic must not be joined, but the left end should be turned back twice and have a button sewn on it. This will keep the elastic from running back. On the other end of the elastic a hem should be made, and a buttonhole loop made on its extreme edge to pass over the button. Each end of elastic must be secured to the garment with a few stitches, but it can be removed easily if it is not desirable to wash it. If strings are to be used instead of elastic, the casings are made in the same way.

Other Casings

Sometimes a small casing is needed on the waist-line at the back of a petticoat or other garment. In this case a strip of material cut on the selvedge threads is necessary, and it should be twice the width of the elastic, tape or ribbon. Top and bottom edges should be turned down narrowly, and rather more at each end. Then the upper and lower edges should be tacked into place and machined close to the fold, but the ends should be left open. If only one string is used, pass it through the casing and sew it through the middle of the strip with an upright row of back stitch or else a large cross stitch. If two strings to cross are used, sew one to each end of the casing before it is applied, then lay the strings flatly over one another, and tack and stitch the casing into place with one string emerging at each end. Be sure to keep clear of the strings when you are machining.

BUTTONHOLED SLOTS FOR RIBBON

These slots are often used round the waist and neck of nightgowns and petticoats. They must of necessity be in single material, and so this must be firm, even though at the same time it may be fine. The slots are always upright, never horizontal. Draw them on the material with pencil and ruler. They should be $\frac{1}{16}$ inch longer than the width of the ribbon. They are usually in pairs about 1 inch apart, leaving about 2 inches between the pairs. The slots must be worked very lightly in buttonhole stitch, but without pulling tightly on the corded edge, and both ends must be the same— either barred or round. On very fine material— say lawn, crêpe-de-chine or silk—the slots may be whipped as in *broderie anglaise* in the following way : Pencil the slot, but do not cut it. Take needle and fine embroidery cotton for lawn, or twisted embroidery silk for silk, and run finely round the mark on both sides. Then cut the slit and work close over-and-over stitches from right to left all round over the running stitches, turning down the extreme edge with the needle as you go along.

SEWING ON STRINGS

If ribbon strings are to be set into the ends of hems, they should be sewn on before the hems are sewn. Arrange the hem, then tack the end of ribbon for ⅜ inch to the inside of the hem and stitch the hem. If hand-stitched, then the ribbon must be felled to the hem at each end, but if machined the line of stitching may be carried up the ends of the hems. When the ribbon is not to be in a hem, but sewn inside the ends of an opening, place the end of the ribbon—right side downward—about ¼ inch from the end of the garment. Run the ribbon to the material, then turn the ribbon over and fold it backward to meet the edge of material. Seam the two together, and then flatten out the seam, after which fell the side edges of the ribbon.

SHOULDER STRAPS

Ribbon or double strips of the garment material are generally employed for the shoulder straps of cami-knickers, petticoats, etc., when these have straight-edged tops. Their position depends on the figure, and should be marked with pins after trying on the garment. Sew them on as described for ribbon strings. The stitches should not show on the right side, so, if the material is thin, it is best to make a small bow of ribbon, or a rosette, to cover any stitches.

Mark the position of the straps, then make a buttonhole slot (vertical) in the garment at each position. If the material is single, it must be backed with small pieces for strength, felling these finely all round. Hem each end of the ribbon and sew a flat button on the under side of each, covered on the right side with a bow or rosette. The button goes through to the inside of the garment.

To Prevent Straps Slipping

On the turnings of each shoulder seam of a frock attach a little strap of double material near the neck. Fasten the other end by means of press studs either to the turnings near the armhole seam, or to the end of the sleeve extender. Pass the petticoat straps under this little strap and you will be spared the discomfort of shoulder straps halfway down the arm.